T0114455

THE PSYCHOLOGY OF FASHION

What do our clothes say about us? How do the clothes we wear affect our moods and emotions? How does the fashion industry encourage us to aspire to look in a certain way?

The Psychology of Fashion offers an insightful introduction to the exciting and dynamic world of fashion in relation to human behaviour, from how clothing can affect our cognitive processes to the way retail environments manipulate consumer behaviour. The book explores how fashion design can impact healthy body image, how psychology can inform a more sustainable perspective on the production and disposal of clothing, and why we develop certain shopping behaviours.

With fashion imagery ever present in the streets, press and media, *The Psychology of Fashion* shows how fashion and psychology can make a positive difference to our lives.

Professor Carolyn Mair is a freelance consultant specialising in the psychology of fashion. She works with educators, clothing brands and media outlets. She pioneered the Masters and Bachelors programmes on the psychology of fashion at London College of Fashion.

THE PSYCHOLOGY OF EVERYTHING

The Psychology of Everything is a series of books which debunk the myths and pseudo-science surrounding some of life's biggest questions.

The series explores the hidden psychological factors that drive us, from our sub-conscious desires and aversions, to the innate social instincts handed to us across the generations. Accessible, informative, and always intriguing, each book is written by an expert in the field, examining how research-based knowledge compares with popular wisdom, and illustrating the potential of psychology to enrich our understanding of humanity and modern life.

Applying a psychological lens to an array of topics and contemporary concerns – from sex to addiction to conspiracy theories – *The Psychology of Everything* will make you look at everything in a new way.

Titles in the series:

For further information about this series please visit www.thepsychologyofeverything.co.uk

THE
PSYCHOLOGY
OF FASHION

CAROLYN MAIR

Routledge
Taylor & Francis Group

LONDON AND NEW YORK

First published 2018
by Routledge
2 Park Square, Milton Park, Abingdon, Oxon OX14 4RN

and by Routledge
711 Third Avenue, New York, NY 10017

Routledge is an imprint of the Taylor & Francis Group, an informa business

British Library Cataloguing-in-Publication Data
A catalogue record for this book is available from the British Library

Library of Congress Cataloging-in-Publication Data
A catalog record for this book has been requested

ISBN: 978-1-138-65866-0 (hbk)
ISBN: 978-1-138-65867-7 (pbk)
ISBN: 978-1-315-62066-4 (eBook)

Typeset in Joanna
by Apex CoVantage, LLC

In loving memory of my mum, Betty.

CONTENTS

ACKNOWLEDGEMENTS

I would like to thank London College of Fashion, University of the Arts London, for their support while I was writing this book and for allowing me the opportunity to establish a new area for the college, the psychology of fashion. I am grateful for the lively discussions with staff and students about psychology and its relevance to their specific areas of interest in fashion and art. Special thanks are due to Becka Fleetwood-Smith MA, who graduated with an MA in psychology for fashion professionals in 2015, and Zoe Shaughnessy, who graduated with an MSc in applied psychology in fashion in 2016, for allowing me to include findings from their masters' projects.

I'm grateful to the editorial team at Routledge, especially Russell George, for their faith in this project, and their guidance and support throughout.

I would also like to thank my partner, Martin, and my children, Jonathan, Louisa and Sophie; my sister, Elaine; and their families, for their encouragement and pride in my achievements, especially in completing this book.

1

INTRODUCTION

OVERVIEW

Welcome to *The Psychology of Fashion*, part of Routledge's Psychology of
Everything series. This book is designed to introduce you to a new
field of applied psychology: the psychology of fashion. The aim of
this emerging sub-discipline of psychology is to develop a deeper
understanding of the reciprocal influence of fashion (and the fashion
industries) and human behaviour and ultimately to use fashion as a
vehicle for enhancing wellbeing.

Many fashion magazines, blogs and consultants tell us that what we
wear says a lot about who we are. According to these commentators,
fashion expresses who we are, our personality and identity, through
nonverbal communication. This intuitive reasoning is appealing, but
while it encourages conversations about these and other psychological concepts, a scientific underpinning is often missing from the argu-
ment. Since launching the sub-discipline of psychology of fashion,
I have been asked many times about the psychology underlying what
particular fashion items or their features say about the wearer. As
you'll discover when you read this book, the answers are not necessarily intuitive.

Although we make judgements about a person based on their
appearance alone in under 1 second, these judgements are often

flawed. Interpretations of the psychological meaning of clothing are influenced not only by the wearer but also by the observer, as well as by the social and cultural context. Nevertheless, our clothing, like other objects, becomes part of our identity and enables us to align with particular groups while separating us from others. We should be aware, however, that others may not make the same associations about our clothing as we do.

You will be used to seeing fashion imagery in the streets, press and media. You might feel differing degrees of confidence about yourself at different times, in different contexts, as a result. These feelings might have affected your self-esteem, mental health and wellbeing. Because of the ubiquitous nature of fashion imagery, you may not even be aware of its influence. You may have heard about the fashion industry's contribution to environmental and social issues and want to find out more – to go beyond simply knowing more to knowing how individuals can do more. These issues, and many more, can be addressed by psychology, the scientific study of human behaviour.

The intentions of this book are to provide an understanding of the reciprocal influences between fashion in its broadest sense and human behaviour, and to motivate you to become more confident in your involvement with fashion and, in doing so, contribute to a more ethical and sustainable industry.

This book is designed for a general audience. There is no assumption of expertise in either fashion or psychology. This chapter provides definitions of fashion and psychology, a rationale for the importance of applying psychology in the context of fashion, a brief history of fashion, an overview of how evidence can be derived in psychology and a road map for the remainder of the book. Finally, some resources for further reading are provided. Let's get started.

DEFINITIONS

Psychology

The *Oxford English Dictionary* defines psychology as "the scientific study of the human mind and its functions, especially those affecting behaviour in a given context" and "the mental characteristics or attitude of a person or group".[1] The British Psychological Society, the professional body for psychologists in the UK, defines psychology as

> the scientific study of the mind and how it dictates and influences behaviour, from communication and memory to thought and emotion. Psychology is . . . concerned with all aspects of behaviour and the thoughts, feelings, and motivations underlying it. It's about understanding what makes people tick and how this understanding can help us address and solve many of the problems in society. As a science, psychology is dedicated to the study of human behaviour through observation, measurement, and testing in order to form conclusions that are based on sound scientific methodology.[2]

According to the British Psychological Society, psychologists are concerned with understanding theories, and ultimately developing and testing them to enable the prediction of outcomes to improve quality of life (see https://beta.bps.org.uk/DiscoverPsychology). The American Psychological Association's definition states:

> Psychology is the study of the mind and behavior. The discipline embraces all aspects of the human experience – from the functions of the brain to the actions of nations, from child development to care for the aged. In every conceivable setting from scientific research centers to mental healthcare services, the understanding of behavior is the enterprise of psychologists.[3]

Fashion

An agreed definition of fashion is elusive. The *Oxford English Dictionary* defines it as a noun, "a popular or the latest style of clothing, hair, decoration, or behaviour", and as a verb, "a manner of doing something".[4] Valerie Steele, an American fashion historian, curator and director of the Museum at the Fashion Institute of Technology, as well as editor of the journal, *Fashion Theory*, defines *fashion* for the purposes of the journal as the cultural construction of the embodied identity.[5] As such, fashion encompasses all forms of 'self-fashioning', including street styles and high fashion. Fashion is commonly understood to refer to the prevailing style of dress or behaviour, with the result that it is characterised by change. Steele argues that fashion attracts attention because of its intimate relationship with the physical body and therefore the identity of the wearer. Tansey Hoskins, in *Stitched Up: The Anti-Capitalist Book of Fashion* (2014), describes how fashion offers a social process of negotiation and navigation which has a "cultivated mystique".[6] She argues that the industry perpetuates the notion that Milan, London, Paris and New York produce fashion, and that everything produced outside these centres is simply apparel or clothing. *Fashion* by definition is related to change and is typically associated with younger groups, whereas *clothing* is used as an umbrella term encompassing functional as well as decorative items. In this book we use the terms interchangeably for ease of reading.

THE IMPORTANCE OF APPLYING PSYCHOLOGY IN THE CONTEXT OF FASHION

Fashion is creative, exciting and dynamic, and because of its nature and inextricably close relationship with the body, the fashion industry manifests many issues which affect us psychologically at individual, societal and global levels.

Clothing is our second skin; it sits next to our bodies and becomes part of our identity. Fashion garments are often described in sensory terms such as vision and touch. The other senses are also important in fashion. Consider the sense of smell for the fragrance and beauty industries, as well as for items made from leather. Sound may be overlooked when thinking of sensory aspects of fashion, but consider the sound of heels on pavement, or the rustle of taffeta. Sensory input is processed in the brain through the psychological phenomenon of perception. In order for sensory stimulation from the environment to be perceived, it needs attention. For interpretation of sensory input to take place, we draw on memory, creativity and communication.

All these are psychological in nature because they take place in the brain. Clothing is also important in terms of functionality and protection, but equally importantly it is the vehicle by which we promote ourselves to others. As a cultural phenomenon, fashion is concerned with meanings and symbols which provide instant visual communication to be interpreted and responded to by those we interact with. Although researchers have found that clothing style can convey qualities such as character, sociability, competence and intelligence, often what is conveyed is different from what was intended because communication in any medium is complex.

Because communication involves many brain processes, it is considered psychological. Interpreting the meaning of any message is complex as there are so many opportunities for distortion of the meaning. As Barnard argues in *Fashion as Communication*, interpreting meaning from fashion or clothing is difficult and fraught with problems.[7] Nevertheless, clothing and fashion can be used in many positive ways to enhance our life chances, self-esteem and wellbeing. Once more, these are psychological constructs.

Fashion is an important global industry employing millions worldwide. The global apparel market (including sub-industries such as menswear, womenswear and sportswear) is valued at US$3 trillion. It accounts for 2% of the world's gross domestic product and employs 57.8 million people across the world, generating an income of more than £26 billion annually in the UK alone.[8] Fascinating as it is to analyse an individual's clothing, fashion is concerned with far more than what we wear. The fashion industry's employees work in many different disciplines, including the obvious ones such as fashion and textile design, textile production, manufacturing, marketing, distribution, retail and visual merchandising, and the less obvious ones, such as computer programming, law, accountancy, copywriting, social media, project management and increasingly psychology.

Because fashion is inherently concerned with human behaviour, it can be considered a form of psychology. Despite this, most of the literature on fashion comes from cultural theorists, fashion historians, sociologists, anthropologists and philosophers; until recently, few psychologists engaged in the debate. Kaiser, in *The Social Psychology of Clothing* (1997), describes psychologists' slow development of interest in clothing and fashion, but, fortunately, times have changed.[9] We are now seeing enthusiasm from the industry for psychological evidence to enable a deeper understanding and better prediction of human behaviour. This evidence can be used to help improve the industry's practices in response to its ethical and social responsibilities.

By now I hope to have convinced you that the application of psychology in the context of fashion is important, but before I move on to an in-depth discussion of this, it seems just to provide a brief history of fashion. Please note that this is not intended to be comprehensive. Rather, it is intended to provide context for the remainder of the book.

A BRIEF HISTORY OF FASHION

Fashion ranges from high couture to high street, but regardless of its origins, fashion is conceived of, produced and sold by people for people. Fashion can be considered a continual process of change over time and over space. In some cases, fashion precedes political change; at other times, it follows it. The globalisation of fashion has resulted in more homogeneous dressing around the world, but it wasn't always this way.

Anthropologists argue that humans began wearing clothes in the Neanderthal period (approximately 200,000–30,000 BCE) when they started using tools made of bone rather than stone. Bone tools enabled Neanderthals to soften skins without tearing them, making them more pliable and more able to be made into clothing. Prior to this, humans had decorated their bodies for rituals and as a sign of status. As body decorations were hidden once humans started wearing clothing, they began to decorate the clothing, which assumed a decorative as well as a functional purpose. Spun, dyed and knotted wild flax fibres found in caves in Georgia, dating back hundreds of thousands of years, are considered to be remnants of clothing made in response to decreasing amounts of body hair and the resulting need to keep warm. Other accounts claim that the need for clothing arose as humans moved from Africa to colder climates and settled in Mesopotamia (present-day Iraq). The Mesopotamians spun and wove wool and made felt and other fibres to produce clothing and footwear such as loin cloths for men and shawls and skirts for women. Even then, wealthy people wore large, elaborate jewellery made of gold and silver and used perfume and cosmetics. According to these accounts, later, as the diaspora spread, the first Egyptian cultures formed along the banks of the Nile. At this time, men and women dressed in light, loose, flowing woollen or linen clothing draped around the body. They cared for and decorated their skin with cosmetics and wore headdresses as status symbols. Similarly, as humans moved to Greece, clothing and jewellery were worn as an indicator of status. Evidence suggests that around 2500 to 1600 BCE, the societies who lived in the Indus Valley, in modern-day Pakistan, created jewellery and wore fine woven, dyed and decorated fabrics draped around their body. Clothing styles hardly changed for centuries across swathes of the populated world. This 'fashion' lasted for centuries and can be seen as late as the Roman Republic, which started in 509 BCE, when wealthy men and women wore togas draped over a tunic, or a cloak over a long dress.

Clothing was similar in the Far East, where for centuries the major-ity of people in China wore a tunic or jacket and loose trousers, while the upper classes wore a long-sleeved, loose-fitting silk robe which fastened either down the middle or across the right side of the chest. Chinese traditional practices for clothing were maintained until Emperor Pu Yi was toppled in 1911 and 'Western' dress was allowed. However, when Mao Tse-tung's government came to power in 1949, the Mao suit – plain trousers and a tunic with a mandarin collar and two pockets on the chest – was worn across China regardless of class. In recent years, China has become one of world's most impor-tant producers of fashion garments and accessories and is increas-ingly influential in terms of design. Chinese design was influential in Japan from the 6th century CE, when many clothing traditions were adopted; like in China, Western dress was not adopted in Japan until the late 19th century.

In medieval Europe, people wore tunics and capes made of rough wool or animal fur. Later, tailors made garments for wealthy people, with women wearing fitted clothing, with lower necklines over corsets which gave an exaggerated shape to the hips and bust. Men wore tunics over leggings and trousers. Velvet, brocade and linen clothing became popular with the wealthy classes at the time of the Renaissance, and during Elizabethan times (1558–1603), clothing for the wealthy became even more elaborate, with ruffled collars, small waists, broad shoulders, puffed sleeves and wide headdresses. After this came the baroque period (1604–1682), which began in France under King Louis XIV and later spread across Europe. Women wore looser, less elaborate gowns, and men wore doublets and utilitarian leather jackets over full, knee-length breeches rather than hose.

Major changes in clothing occurred during the Georgian and Regency periods because of the Industrial Revolution (1760–1840), when new manufacturing processes were developed, hand-production methods were replaced by machines, water power was harnessed more efficiently, and use of steam power increased. As a result, during the Georgian period (1714–1830), fashion became increasingly important for indicating status. Clothing was characterised by expensively tailored garments in lace and silk brocade. Both men and women wore tall, powdered wigs and high-heeled shoes. Women's dresses featured panniers to widen the silhouette, and men wore plain coats with tails and long, tight breeches. After this, fashion became simpler again. During the Regency period (1811–1837), women wore simple, draped dresses without corsets, tied at the waist; men wore pantaloons and tall boots. Until the Industrial Revolution, clothing and therefore fashion trends had been created by the royalty and copied by dressmakers for their wealthy clients. Poor people and peasants wore hand-me-downs or made their own.

The Industrial Revolution led to a surplus of rural workers seeking employment in industry and a better standard of living in cities. Many people who had lived in rural areas with their extended families moved to cities to live among strangers. In such situations, where we interact with strangers, we have little information other than appearance to use to infer identity, class and so on. Consequently, that which had previously been the preserve of wealthy people, 'fashion', became more important for more people. Yet, despite increased accessibility and demand, fashionable clothing remained the preserve of the wealthy until the treadle sewing machine, invented by Singer in 1869, made mass production of clothing a reality. The increased disposable income of the new middle classes in industrialised cities led to an increased demand for goods. Retail stores opened in cities to meet this need, and marketing strategies encouraged consumerism as an essential element self-worth. This extended to consumption for appearance management, and by the end of the 19th century, fashion magazines were being published in New York and Philadelphia.

Ordinary women and men were becoming more aware of fashion and the notion of being fashionable. It was during this time that the notion of conspicuous consumption was developed by Thorstein Veblen and described in his 1899 work, *Theory of the Leisure Class: An Economic Study in the Evolution of Institutions*.[10] During Queen Victoria's reign, fashion became far more accessible. To meet demand, fashion production became faster, and working conditions deteriorated. The tragic death of 146 workers trapped by fire at the Triangle Shirtwaist Company in New York City in 1911 prompted the introduction of legislation requiring regular hours, paid leave, sick benefits and better working conditions. Although this benefited workers, fashion became less elaborate. Sadly, more than a century later, we are still witnessing disasters at fashion's sweatshops.

In the 1920s, women become more liberated. They discarded their restrictive clothing and adopted the androgynous 'flapper' style. This era is considered the golden age of French fashion, when designers, including Jean Patou and Coco Chanel, designed sporty, athletic looks for men and women. After the Great Depression of 1929–1939, the 'flapper' look was replaced by long, flowing dresses influenced by French designers Coco Chanel, Madeleine Vionnet and Jeanne Lanvin, as well as Italian designer, Elsa Schiaparelli. During World War II, when resources for clothing were limited, clothing needed to be produced more efficiently, and the UK government's utility clothing scheme was developed. This comprised a limited range of garments, styles and fabrics which guaranteed quality and value for money. In autumn 1941, it became compulsory for all utility fabrics and garments to be marked 'CC41', which stood for "Civilian Clothing 1941". Additional austerity measures introduced in 1942 and 1943 by the British Board of Trade made further savings in labour and manufacturing costs. In men's clothing, for example, lapels became narrower, single breasted jackets replaced double breasted ones, turn-ups were banned, and pockets were reduced. But style remained an important factor for clothing, so the Board of Trade established the Incorporated Society of London Fashion Designers in 1942 to counter the potential lack of style and differentiation in clothing. Eight leading fashion designers designed an attractive, stylish and varied range of utility clothing which was economical and within the austerity regulations.

After World War II, haute couture become popular, influenced by Christian Dior's 'New Look' silhouette of longer, fuller skirts; smooth, rounded shoulders; and tiny, fitted waists. In addition, as a result of new technology, synthetic and easy-care fabrics were used to create a less structured, more casual look. Simultaneously, social changes allowed young people in their teens to stay in education, which led to the development of the 'beat generation' and the 'beatnik', exemplified by students who wore the 'beat' (beaten) look of plain dark clothing and sunglasses. In parallel, working teenage boys opted for suits, ties and button-down shirts. Working teenage girls accentuated their hourglass silhouette with full skirts over petticoats with tight cardigans or sweaters. Others in the 1950s preferred the 'Teddy Boy' look inspired by American rock and roll idols; they wore leather jackets, skinny ties, tight trousers and brightly coloured socks. For the first time, teenagers wore clothes that were different from their parents' clothes and thus became influential in fashion. After the beat generation, students opted for the 'preppie' look of sweaters and T-shirts with skirts or blue jeans.

International fashion trends were influenced by the London pop music scene in the 1960s, with the 'mod' look created by British designers Mary Quant, Zandra Rhodes and Jean Muir. The 'mod' look was uncluttered, with geometric shapes for women and a sleek, sharp style for men. Mods have been described as lower-class dandies who desired upward mobility and an escape from working-class life. While appearance mattered hugely to the mods, who cruised around on scooters, their opposites, rockers, wore leather, rode motor bikes and were perceived as tough, masculine types. During this period, London became a fashion hub as boutiques for young consumers opened across the city. However, by the late 1960s, the desire for mass-produced fashion was being replaced by the desire for less materialism and a more natural lifestyle. The 'hippy' movement, which began on the west coast of America, spread to the UK fashion scene and brought with it loose and bright clothing, based on styles from Eastern ethnicities. Leading designers in the UK at that time were Ossie Clark, Jean Muir, Thea Porter and Zandra Rhodes. The early 1970s brought more variety in fashion, influenced by music, and although the hippy look remained, young urbanites opted for a more androgynous silhouette with platform shoes and high-waisted trousers and a glamorous look in discos. Later that decade, the punk movement was characterised by torn, black clothing held together with straps, zippers, studs, safety-pins and chains, worn with work boots or Doc Martins. Hair was dyed into unnatural colours and styled in Mohican spikes. The 1980s saw a dramatic shift from the punk and hippy look. Women's styles featured shoulder pads, short skirts, leg warmers, stretch ski pants and over-sized shirts.

The 1990s saw an increase in the rave culture, with England, Germany and America creating new genres of dance music and fashion. Neon colours, glow sticks, short skirts and crop tops were the uniform for clubbing. In addition to new movements in music and fashion, the 1990s saw a lot of movement in the fashion industry. For example, after Isabella Blow, a stylist for *Vogue*, saw Alexander McQueen's graduation collection in 1992, he was featured in *Vogue*'s November issue. John Galliano became head of the French couture house Givenchy and then replaced Gianfranco Ferré at Dior. McQueen went to Givenchy, and Michael Kors to Céline. Stella McCartney took over at Chloé, while Marc Jacobs went to Louis Vuitton, and Alber

Elbaz moved to Guy Laroche before becoming Yves Saint Laurent's head of the ready-to-wear collections. Rapid advances in technology in the 1990s meant we were seeing more images and video footage of designers, models and fashion in general. People aspired to the life-styles portrayed by designer brands, and the supermodels of the time were shown alongside the new faces of young unknowns, including Kate Moss, who was chosen by photographer Mario Testino because he refused to pay the prices demanded by the likes of top models Linda Evangelista and Cindy Crawford.

Since this time, although materials have developed, fashion has recycled styles from previous decades. In the 2000s, many fashion styles emerged from young people in the lower socio-economic groups who belonged to subcultures or 'style tribes'; these styles trickled down through celebrities to the wealthy young people who wished to look 'cool'. In addition, high-end fashion, couture and luxury, once the preserve of royals and the wealthy, became acces-sible anywhere to anyone with an internet connection and a credit card. Designer outfits worn on the red carpet for celebrity events are copied directly and available in high street stores and even in your home within hours.

This fast fashion has changed the way fashion is designed, pro-duced and consumed, to the detriment of all three aspects. Designers are pressured to work much faster and produce more collections, which affects the design process and the mental health of design-ers. In addition, although many consumers are becoming educated about the environmental problems resulting from the fashion supply chain and manufacturing process, they still tend to buy more than they need. Furthermore, many consumers dispose of unwanted items carelessly, sometimes without ever wearing them. Fortunately, some individuals are becoming increasingly concerned about the detrimen-tal effects of unethical fashion production and consumption on work-ers, consumers and the environment. As a result, they are becoming activists for a more sustainable fashion industry.

The fashion industry has grown at a rate of 5.5% annually and is now worth an estimated US$2.4 trillion per year globally, but recent years have been especially turbulent for the global economy, and certainty seems a long way off. Like in many industries, growth in the fashion industry is slowing, according to the McKinsey Global Fashion Index, reported in the *State of Fashion* report (2017).[11] The three main reasons for the decline are cited as the global economy, consumer behaviour and the fashion business model. Consumers are become more demanding, more discerning and less predictable in their purchasing behaviour. An evidence-based understanding has never been more needed.

The increasing interest in wearable tech for monitoring of health and wellbeing and for decorative fashion is driving innovation and change. The technological developments of 3D printing and augmented and virtual reality are being combined with technology that monitors our physical responses and motivates us to form new habits and achieve a better quality of life. Psychologists understand not only behaviour and ways to implement behaviour change but also user experience and engagement.

Clothing has developed from being purely functional to being one of the world's most important and fascinating industries. As humans have developed and their basic needs are met, they experience greater motivation for belonging, esteem and self-actualisation. Fashion and fashion-related products can satisfy these needs in some while driving motivation to belong in others. Humans are involved in every aspect of fashion: design, production, manufacture, advertising and marketing, visual merchandising, retail, consumption and disposal.

Fashion matters beyond what our clothes say about us. Fashion affects how we view ourselves and others, our self and identity, and how we navigate our worlds. To better understand the role and value of applying psychology in the context of fashion, we now provide a brief overview of how psychologists derive and interpret data.

HOW EVIDENCE IN PSYCHOLOGY IS DERIVED AND INTERPRETED

Call it clothing, apparel or fashion, what we wear is without doubt an important aspect of human experience. However, there has been a general lack of interest in investigating fashion from psychologists (other than a few exceptional social psychologists). The evolving discipline of psychology of fashion demands the application of existing theories in novel contexts and the proposing of interpretations tentatively as hypotheses. These will be tested over the coming years to support or refute existing theory. As a science, psychology emphasises rigour and seeks an evidence-based approach considered through a critical-thinking lens. Because of the scarcity of evidence-based psychology in the context of fashion, we need to apply existing theories to hypothesise and test potential outcomes. Psychological research is typically defined as 'pure' or 'applied'. Pure research is lab-based and is used to inform applied research. Applied research tests models and theories in situ (as opposed to in the lab) derived from pure research and is used to improve pure research by making it more ecologically valid (applicable beyond the lab situation). Psychologists working in industry or other 'applied' settings might be employed to work with staff to understand and improve their experience and quality of life. Other psychologists apply design thinking to develop inclusive, creative innovations that help people live better, while others work in law, music, medicine, media and even fashion. Of course, psychologists also work in the traditional areas of clinical psychology, counselling, sports and exercise, health, education, forensics, and occupational/industry psychology. Regardless of context, psychologists apply theories and models to help others by increasing knowledge, improving performance or enhancing wellbeing.

Psychologists typically describe themselves as trained in one or another of the core sub-disciplines in psychology. For example, cognitive psychologists work to understand brain processes including sensation and perception, emotion, communication, memory, thinking and reasoning, creativity, and problem-solving and decision-making. All these topics are relevant if we are to develop a better understanding of the reciprocal influence of fashion and human behaviour. Social psychologists aim to understand and explain how the attitudes, thoughts, feelings and behaviour of individuals are influenced by the actual, imagined or implied presence of others. Social psychologists tend to take an interactional approach to understanding human behaviour in social contexts. This emphasises a person's cognitive and personality factors as well as the immediate social situation. Developmental psychologists study behaviour across the lifespan. Many people consider the psychology of fashion to be concerned mainly with consumer behaviour and marketing. However, consumer behaviour and marketing cannot exist without the underpinning of the 'basic' sub-disciplines of psychology, including biological, cognitive, social and developmental. In many cases, consumer behaviour also requires input from applied areas of psychology, including, but not limited to, organisational and business psychology. Psychologists are increasingly working with or as neuroscientists, striving to understand where the neural correlates of particular behaviours lie within the brain. This exciting work is beyond the scope of this book, but if you are interested, there are many excellent texts on this subject.

People are interested in psychology for many different reasons. Psychology allows us to understand why we do the things we do. This enables us to predict and, ultimately, change behaviour. In psychology, the outcomes of observations and interventions are interpreted in terms of probability, not certainty. The application of psychology requires critical thinking because human behaviour is complex and unpredictable. Taking a scientific approach means that samples (subpopulations) must be representative of the population of interest and that each sample is drawn randomly from that population. This means that everyone in the population has an equal chance of being selected. Using random sampling from the population of interest and selecting a large enough group allow us to make generalisations from the analysis of the data we collect. However, interpretations are always articulated in terms of probability or likelihood and therefore are always tentative. Psychologists apply critical thinking to scrutinise methods, results and theories in order to derive a better understanding and eventually establish new theories through iterative hypothesis testing.

Psychologists analyse the responses they collect through observations which depend on many factors, including whether they wish to gain deep and rich meaning from a small number of individuals or whether they wish to generalise to an entire population. In the first case, they would use qualitative methods, and in the second case, they would use quantitative methods. An in-depth coverage of psychological research methods is beyond the scope of this text. Therefore, if you're interested in learning more about designing, analysing and interpreting data in research studies in psychology, please refer to the many research methods texts available (see the suggestions for further reading at the end of this book). Despite psychology being one of the most popular subjects to study at university, public understanding remains riddled with myths and misunderstandings. Some common examples are the claims that 'learning styles' for enhanced performance exist, that we use only 10% of our brain, that people are right-brained or left-brained and that psychologists can read minds. Interested readers are encouraged to read Christian Jarrett's 2014 work, *Great Myths of the Brain*, which discusses popular myths about the human brain.

ROAD MAP

This chapter has provided information that underpins the remainder of the book: definitions, the rationale for the importance of psychology in fashion, a brief history of fashion and an overview of how evidence is derived and interpreted in psychology. The remainder of the book is organised as follows: Chapter 2, "Wellbeing in the Fashion Industry", introduces the concepts of positive psychology and psychological wellbeing. It looks at mental health in the fashion industry as experienced by fashion designers and models. The focus of Chapter 3, "The Influence of Fashion on Body Image and 'Beauty'", focuses on body image, beauty and cosmetic interventions, the influence of social media, and objectification. Chapter 4, "Fashion, Self and Identity", is concerned with the concepts of self and identity; it discusses theories of self and identity and their relation to fashion and inclusivity, as well as social groups and fashion. Chapter 5, "Fashion Consumption", deals with shopping for fashion, sustainable fashion and clothing for wellbeing. Chapter 6, "Fashion and Behaviour", is concerned with the reasons behind our clothing choices, the messages that our clothes communicate and the reciprocal relationship of body and mind. Finally, Chapter 7 concludes the book by bringing it all together and proposing what's next for the fashion industries. At the end of the book is a selection of suggestions for further reading.

2

WELLBEING IN THE FASHION INDUSTRY

OVERVIEW

Our clothing serves many purposes beyond functionality and shelter: it conveys symbolic meaning; meets the demands of individual taste, modesty and cultural expectations; and can display social status and gender preference. However, at a broader level, clothing, fashion and the fashion industry can also influence our mental health and psychological wellbeing, concepts that seem to be on everyone's agenda these days. This chapter introduces a growing area of interest, positive psychology, and one of its components, psychological wellbeing, and discusses reports of mental health issues among fashion designers and models.

POSITIVE PSYCHOLOGY AND PSYCHOLOGICAL WELLBEING

Professor Martin Seligman is known as the psychologist who moved psychology from the scientific study of psychopathology, what's wrong with individuals, to the scientific study of "positive subjective experience, positive individual traits, and positive institutions".[1] Positive psychology focuses on individuals' strengths, rather than their weaknesses, and aims to enable all individuals to be the best they can be. It is generally understood to have two theoretical perspectives: hedonic and eudaemonic. The hedonic approach is also known as subjective wellbeing, defined as pleasure attainment, pain avoidance and satisfaction with life in general. This is greatest when there is little or no discrepancy between the present state and the perceived ideal situation. The eudaemonic approach focuses on psychological wellbeing, defined in terms of meaning and the degree to which a person is fully functioning. Research has found that when an individual subjectively experiences positive moods, this leads to more sociability, better health, greater success, improved self-regulation and helping behaviour, enhanced creativity and divergent thinking. In addition, happy people are more likely to finish unpleasant tasks, they are more systematic and attentive, and they live longer. Positive psychology and wellbeing are factors that vary throughout life; however, they are rarely studied in relation to fashion, and therefore we know very little about the influence of fashion on wellbeing.

In affluent societies, survival is no longer the only priority; boosting quality of life has become increasingly important. In addition, societies are becoming more individualistic, as people are concerned with themselves and close family members only, as opposed to collectivistic societies, in which people feel a reciprocal sense of belonging and loyalty to larger in-groups. Seeking an enhanced quality of life coupled with an individualistic approach means there is more demand for greater personal happiness. This has led to increased interest in wellbeing among psychologists, educators, governments and the public. In psychology, wellbeing is encompassed in the sub-discipline of *positive psychology*, a term coined by Abraham Maslow and published in the journal *Psychological Review* in 1943. Interested readers are encouraged to read *A Theory of Human Motivation*.[2]

The positive psychology movement became influential in 1999 when Seligman, as president of the American Psychological Association, proclaimed that psychology had achieved many of its aims in helping the 30% of the population suffering mental ill-health. He argued that the majority of the population were being neglected by psychologists. Of this majority, only a few appeared to be flourishing, while the remainder were languishing. Seligman envisaged the future role of psychology as enabling everyone to improve their mental health. Seligman's scientific investigations have led to findings demonstrating that the most satisfied and positive people were those who had identified and fully used their own character strengths such as humanity, temperance and persistence. Seligman argues that positive psychology has three dimensions: the Pleasant Life, the Good Life and the Meaningful Life, which explain how the individualistic and altruistic approaches combine to optimise human flourishing.[3]

The *Character Strengths and Virtues* (CSV) handbook (2004) identifies and classifies positive psychological traits in a similar way to the *Diagnostic and Statistical Manual of Mental Disorders* (DSM), which identifies and classifies mental pathology. The CSV identifies six classes of virtues which have historical bases in the majority of cultures and which could lead to increased happiness when developed. Each virtue is the basis of character strengths, as follows:

1 Wisdom and knowledge: creativity, curiosity, open-mindedness, love of learning, perspective and innovation
2 Courage: bravery, persistence, integrity, vitality and zest
3 Humanity: love, kindness and social intelligence
4 Justice: citizenship, fairness and leadership
5 Temperance: forgiveness and mercy, humility, prudence and self-control
6 Transcendence: appreciation of beauty and excellence, gratitude, hope, humour and spirituality

Seligman argues that the Pleasant Life can be achieved if we savour and appreciate basic pleasures such as companionship, the natural environment and those things that satisfy our bodily needs. We can progress from the Pleasant Life to the Good Life through discovering and using our unique virtues and strengths. The final stage, the Meaningful Life, is described as one in which we further enhance our unique strengths by contributing to the happiness of others. In doing so we develop a deep sense of fulfilment by using our unique strengths for a purpose greater than ourselves.

Psychosocial influences on mental health and wellbeing

Despite or because of the increased interest in psychological wellbeing, reports of mental health problems are increasing worldwide. Individuals are becoming more aware of their own mental health and are being encouraged to speak up when life becomes stressful and impacts their daily functioning. The Mental Health Foundation reports that depression, anxiety and drug use are the primary drivers of disability worldwide, impacting length and quality of life.[4] Moreover, one in four people in the UK will experience a mental health problem each year. Despite a concerted effort to make support available and to encourage individuals to speak out about their mental health issues, the World Health Organization reports that between 35% and 50% of people with severe mental health problems in developed countries, and 76% to 85% of people in developing countries, receive no treatment, and up to 80% of people who report having mental health problems do not seek support.[5] The Adult Psychiatric Morbidity Survey of Mental Health and Wellbeing, England (2014), found that 37% of adults aged 16–74 with conditions such as anxiety or depression were accessing mental health treatment.[6] We know that every week one in six adults experiences symptoms such as anxiety or depression, and 20% of adults have considered taking their own life at some point. Almost 50% of adults believe that they have had a diagnosable mental health problem, yet only a third have received a diagnosis.

Mental health problems are being reported increasingly across the age span and across socio-economic strata and ethnic groups. Clearly, psychological, cultural, social and socio-economic factors influence mental health. Statistics show that people receiving financial support from social services are more likely to have mental health issues, and this same population may not have the physical or financial resources to find mental health support.

Women between the ages of 16 and 24 are almost three times more likely than men of the same age to experience a common mental health problem. Women have higher rates of self-harm, bipolar disorder and post-traumatic stress disorder. However, these figures may disguise the actual data because men are less likely to report mental health issues.

Of those individuals with mental health issues, 1.6 million report an eating disorder. Evidence shows that a range of biological, psychological and physical risk factors, including body dissatisfaction, perfectionism, genetics, puberty and environmental factors, put individuals at risk for disordered eating. The risk increases fourfold for female college students.[7] Although there may be varied physical and psychological aetiologies for eating disorders, one of the most influential is society's obsession with slenderness. Research has found a relationship between increased television viewing and eating disorders, lower levels of appearance satisfaction and higher levels of internalisation about appearance value, and drive for thinness. The slender, or even thin, ideal is currently considered an essential component of beauty, success, health and control over one's life. Internalisation of the thin ideal predicts increased body dissatisfaction, which can lead to dieting and eating disorders. However, the degree to which individuals are affected by these pressures depends on whether or not they are internalised. Therefore, despite the evidence presented, the pressure towards thinness and exposure to the thin ideal do not necessarily always lead to negative outcomes. Individuals can be active and deliberate in their level of engagement with and internalisation of such images. Furthermore, sociocultural aspects need to be taken into account. Many psychological theories attempt to address this.

Social cognitive theory proposes that we acquire knowledge through observing the behaviour of others within the context of social interactions, experiences and outside media influence and copy that behaviour depending on the outcome. However, our cognitive processes are also shaped by our social and cultural context. Therefore, disordered eating can result from internalisation of pressures from parents and friends as well as media. Social comparison theory describes how we are motivated to gain accurate and positive self-evaluations through comparing ourselves to others for self-enhancement.[8] Gratifications theory is concerned with understanding why and how people actively seek out and use specific media to satisfy specific needs.[9] It discusses how users deliberately choose media that will satisfy their needs, enhance their knowledge and social interactions and provide relaxation, diversion or escape. Like social cognitive theory, it acknowledges the role of free will, arguing that audience members are not passive consumers of media but have power over what media they consume and how they interpret and integrate it into their own lives. Objectification theory describes how our self-perceptions and our perceptions of how others perceive our body are shaped by the degree to which we are treated as an object.[10] Self-objectification occurs when individuals look upon themselves as objects to be evaluated by others. This can result in anxiety, which is defined as unpleasant feelings of dread about anticipated events.

Anxiety is often accompanied by physical and psychological reactions and can lead to withdrawal from situations which have provoked anxiety in the past. Anxiety can be a short-term state or a long-term trait. Women experience more anxiety about their bodies than do men, but this is not surprising given that females are judged on their appearance from infancy. Appearance anxiety is manifested by concern with self-monitoring, checking and adjusting one's appearance. Many recent fashion styles do little to alleviate this. Safety anxiety refers to the concern women have about their appearance to maintain their safety. Shockingly, some male rapists justify their actions by claiming that physically attractive women are threatening, arguing that their actions were in retaliation. Researchers have found that rape victims who were considered more attractive were assigned greater blame for their own rape than those victims perceived as less attractive.

Although individuals are beginning to speak out about their mental health issues, and more support is becoming available, stigma surrounding the disclosure of mental health problems remains. Individuals may refuse to seek help for many complex reasons including shame, fear or concern about being judged as inadequate. In addition, they may not recognise that they have symptoms of poor mental health and therefore may not believe that they should seek help. Furthermore, because poor mental health is often accompanied by feelings of hopelessness, individuals may believe that nothing can help them, so why seek support. If you know anyone affected by any of the issues in this book, please encourage them to seek help. The British Psychological Society[11] and other organisations concerned with mental health emphasise the importance of speaking out and listening.

One aim of applying psychology in the context of fashion is to highlight the existence of such issues and generate collaborative interventions to help solve them. Fashion has the power to contribute to improving mental health, not only for its workers but also for its consumers. Many are calling for enhanced awareness of and education about the importance of mental health and wellbeing. One outcome of this is psychologists' exploration of human behaviour with regard to the fashion industries.

MENTAL HEALTH OF WORKERS IN THE FASHION INDUSTRY

We often hear claims of a correlation between creativity and mental health issues, but a 2008 study which investigated this relationship did not find a correlation.[12] The study investigated the relationship between the creative process and psychopathological and personality characteristics in a sample of 100 artists from a range of disciplines, but not fashion. Results showed that the artists scored higher on deep absorption, focus on present experience, and sense of pleasure and were more open, overly trusting and easily intimate with others compared with the norm. They scored higher on the personality traits of Openness to Experience and Neuroticism. The former involves six dimensions – active imagination, aesthetic sensitivity, attentiveness to feelings, preference for variety, willingness to experiment and intellectual curiosity – and has positive relationships with creativity, intelligence, knowledge and absorption. This could explain why creative individuals often find themselves in the psychological state of 'flow' during their practice. In addition, people high in openness are motivated to seek new experiences and to engage in self-examination. Interestingly, high scores on Openness tend to be unrelated to symptoms of mental disorders. However, individuals who score high on Neuroticism are often *self-conscious and shy* and are more likely to experience anxiety, envy, anger, guilt and depressed mood as they respond poorly to stressors. Interestingly, as creative types also score high on Neuroticism and Openness to Experience, this particular combination of traits could potentially identify a creative individual. Although this study did not look at creative individuals in the fashion industry, it is clear that the fashion industry is attractive for creative types. And although the association between creativity and poor mental health in general is not supported in the literature, individuals working in a creative job are reportedly 25% more likely to experience poor mental health.

The link between fashion (and other creative industries) and mental health is complex, and it is unknown whether these industries actually contribute to mental health issues, or whether those with existing mental health issues are drawn to the creative industries. The fashion industry does not have a particularly good track record for caring about their workers. Many employees are subject to unique pressures that can leave them vulnerable to developing mental health issues or that can exacerbate mental health issues. The discrepancy between research findings and reality could be an artefact of multiple factors such as inadequate definitions of creativity and mood disorders, reliance on anecdotal and autobiographical or biographical sources, and lack of control groups. In addition, the range of types of creativity studied to date has been narrow and typically focused on musicians and artists rather than designers. Despite the evidence for a relationship between creativity and mental health being inconclusive, many incidences of mental health issues in employees across the fashion industry have been reported. The fashion industry employs people in a range of jobs, from designers to machinists, buyers to models. It is beyond the scope of this book to write about the mental health of employees in each sector. Rather, we focus on the high-profile roles of designers and models.

Although creative types might score highly on two personality traits, there is not a single personality profile for fashion designers; some are quiet and unassuming, while others are outgoing and flamboyant. Compare Phoebe Philo, Christopher Bailey and Dries Van Noten with John Galliano and Jean Paul Gaultier. By definition, fashion is about change. When something becomes fashionable, it is out of fashion. Fashion emphasises novelty and continuous reinvention. Increasingly, designers are required to produce more collections each year. This means there is no respite between collections, and little time to reflect and recover. Therefore, in order to meet industry demands, employees work very long hours, often without breaks, which creates a challenging and stressful environment. Ultimately, this impacts the workers' mental health. The fast pace, long hours, competitive nature and high standards demanded in the fashion industries mean that its workers may be more vulnerable to poor mental health than others.

Despite the lack of conclusive evidence for the existence of a relationship between creativity and mental health, a connection has been demonstrated through the increasing numbers of creatives presenting with mental health issues. Sadly, many high-profile fashion professionals have reported mental health issues, and others have taken their own lives. In 2010, the British designer Alexander McQueen took his own life at the age of 40. McQueen was formerly chief designer at Givenchy from 1996 to 2001, before creating his own eponymous label. He was awarded the British Designer of the Year award four times (in 1996, 1997, 2001 and 2003) and the Council of Fashion Designers of America's International Designer of the Year award in 2003. McQueen's workload was believed to have had a direct effect on his mental state. Three years before his untimely death, McQueen's friend and mentor, Isabella Blow, had taken her own life. Sadly, these are not isolated incidents of poor mental health among high-profile fashion professionals.

Yves Saint Laurent's drug use has been well-documented, as has Galliano's mental health breakdown. Yet, at the same time as Galliano was suffering, Dior launched a perfume called Addict. This does nothing other than glamorise mental health problems and shows a complete disregard for the potentially devastating professional and psychological outcomes of poor mental health. Marc Jacobs claims he needed rehab after continued drinking and partying with other fashion professionals. Alber Elbaz left Lanvin after 14 years because of the fashion industry's relentless pace, which he claimed crushed creativity and exposed designers to the necessity of finding other ways of keeping up. Fortunately, designers and underweight models are beginning to speak out as the increasingly fast pace of fashion demands takes its toll.

An additional reason for poor mental health among fashion designers is that they sometimes go from living in relative obscurity to being responsible for billion-dollar businesses relatively suddenly. In these cases, it is likely that there will be psychological issues to deal with which may or may not be recognised by the designer, and seeking and finding support may not be a viable option. Evidence to suggest such pressures do exist is rare, but in investigations into post-fame mortality rates in a sample of more than 1000 pop stars, Bellis et al. found that the pop music industry, like the fashion industry, is frequently characterised by many high-profile deaths and indulgence in high-risk behaviours.[13] They argued that very little support is in place to support newly famous musicians, whose most risky period is 3 to 25 years post fame. If they survive this period, the risk of pre-mature death diminishes.

Given the lack of literature on either mental health or premature mortality within the fashion industry, it may be safe to assume a general lack of awareness of the need for psychological support for fashion professionals, especially during their newly famous years. One of fashion's most established and revered leaders, Karl Lagerfeld, compares a career in fashion to bullfighting. He argues that those unable to run should not enter the bullring. American designer Rick Owens is also unsympathetic. For him, being busy is being happy. While this may be true for some people in the short term, in the long term constant high-level demands on time and mental resources are not sustainable. Something has to 'give', and often the first resource to do this is the individual's mental health.

The fashion industry's unrealistic ideal of physical perfection is at odds with good mental and physical health. Striving for this unrealistic ideal can exacerbate pressures for those working in the industry as well as for its consumers. As a result, models fare particularly badly in terms of mental health despite the glamorous lifestyle associated with this profession. The requirement for 'perfection', coupled with the demanding social agenda that accompanies working as a model in fashion, makes it easy to understand why poor mental health and burnout occur. Often vulnerable young girls and boys, desperate to enter the modelling profession, may be expected to consent to particular activities which they find unpleasant and uncomfortable, but because they lack experience, confidence or the courage to refuse, they consent. This can result in lingering feelings of shame and guilt which may develop into mental health problems.

One model who has spoken out about her damaging experiences is Rosie Nelson. When Ms Nelson was told by a model agency to lose weight, she did. When she returned to the agency having lost the weight, she was told to "slim down to the bone". As a result, she started a petition which was signed by more than 113,000 people in the UK to draw Parliament's attention to the issues faced in the modelling industry. Since this, Ms Nelson has become an activist for better health care in the modelling industry. Fashion commentator Prof Caryn Franklin, MBE, argues that in addition to the need to be very slim, models are now required to be taller than in previous years. Yet, despite this, the clothing that models are expected to wear is the same tiny size as previously. Thus, there is even greater pressure for models to weigh less to meet the normalised ideal.

A ground-breaking initiative to support the mental health and wellbeing of fashion models, the Model Sanctuary, was set up by model Erin O'Connor in 2008, following the British Fashion Council's 2007 Model Health Inquiry report.[14] Sadly, this was forced to close in 2012, but it has been reincarnated as the Model Zone by the British Fashion Council, which describes it as an exclusive space for models to rest, eat, drink and receive treatments during London Fashion Weeks, between their castings, catwalk shows and presentations.

Fortunately, after years of ignoring activism and facing criticism, the fashion industry has taken steps to ban very young and very thin models. Fashion conglomerates Kering and LVMH, whose brands include Alexander McQueen, Balenciaga, Céline, Christopher Kane, Dior, Louis Vuitton and Stella McCartney, have signed a charter to improve the working conditions for models. From September 2017, models must be a US size 2 (UK size 6) or larger. Models below the age of 16 will be banned from photo shoots and runway shows. Models between the ages of 16 and 18 will not be allowed to work between 10pm and 6am and must be accompanied by a parent or guardian.

Of course, one size does not fit all when it comes to models. Some models thrive in the pressured environment, while others go on to even more successful careers in related industries (for example, Cara Delavigne's career move to acting). Others start their own fashion brands as designers. This does not reduce the risk of experiencing mental health issues given the additional pressures brought by fame compounded by the ephemeral nature of many aspects of the fashion industry.

SUMMARY

Positive psychology is an approach aimed at improving wellbeing for everyone. It is based on humanist and Buddhist philosophies and has been found to be a powerful tool for enhancing satisfaction with life in general. Psychological wellbeing is a component of positive psychology and comprises two components: hedonic and eudaemonic. Interest in wellbeing has escalated over the past decade and with this has come a drive for speaking out about one's own mental health and seeking support. Despite or because of this, reports of mental health issues are increasing across all populations, not least within the fashion industry. In this chapter we discussed published material that profiles the mental health of a few high-profile fashion designers and models and argue that the high-profile fashion and other creative professionals who speak out about their mental health are positive role models for their 'fans', who may be encouraged to also speak out as a result. Although the fashion industry has been rather slow in managing the mental health and wellbeing of its employees, there are signs of improvement. Achieving this in an industry which depends on novelty and change is challenging. Unsurprisingly, the influence of fashion on wellbeing extends beyond its workforce to its consumers. The next chapter discusses how fashion impacts consumers' wellbeing in relation to their appearance.

3

THE INFLUENCE OF FASHION ON BODY IMAGE AND 'BEAUTY'

OVERVIEW

Many factors in the fashion industry affect its consumers, who spend increasing amounts of time seeking inspiration and information online and in traditional media when they select and buy fashion items, including cosmetics. While these activities are intended to support informed decision-making, they also offer opportunities for increased exposure to fashion imagery, which can lead to appearance concerns.

BODY IMAGE

The beauty of the human body has always been considered important in human society, but what is considered beautiful has changed throughout history and across cultures. Because people want to match the ideal of their time and culture, the fashionable body emerges out of the *zeitgeist*. Our external appearance affects our lives in complex ways.

The term *body image* was first defined in 1935 by Paul Schilder, an Austrian psychiatrist and pupil of Sigmund Freud, as "a person's perception of the aesthetics or sexual attractiveness of their own body".[1]

More recent definitions argue that a person's body image is a product of personal experiences, personality and a variety of social and cultural forces and comprises a cognitive and an emotional component. The former is concerned with perceptions of the appearance of one's body, the latter with responses to those perceptions. Body image can be distorted when we focus disproportionately on the size or shape of our body and perceive it to be incongruous with society's standard, inferior to others' bodies and different from the 'ideal' represented in the media.

Fashion enables us to accentuate or conceal certain aspects of our body and associate ourselves with particular social or ethnic groups. However, this freedom to express ourselves fully through clothing is influenced in part by the attitude we hold towards our body, such as how satisfied we are with its weight and shape, with the texture and tone of our skin. Given the impact of social and cultural influences, how we feel about our bodies can be considered indicative of cultural ideology, social relations and personal activities. In this sense, bodies become signifiers of individuals as social beings within a larger cultural and historical context.

Grogan explains how the fashion and cosmetics industries reinforce and normalise the thin body ideal by representing women as much thinner than the actual population through consistent use of underweight and digitally altered images of models and underweight actresses.[2] Only 1 in 40,000 women meets the requirements for a model's size and shape, according to feminist Naomi Wolf. In 1991, Wolf argued that this ideal of the female body is a "myth, unrealistic and impossible to attain", and, consequently, striving to attain it can lead to feelings of shame, poor body satisfaction and low self-esteem as well as a life-long journey of diets and exercise regimes.[3]

Opportunities for exposure to fashion imagery have increased considerably as a result of technological advances since Wolf's paper and even more so since the development of social media. Because of its ubiquity, the unrealistic ideal becomes the norm to which we compare ourselves and by which we assess or judge our own worth. Wolf's claims are supported by evidence which shows that while girls and young women are generally considered the populations most likely to be influenced negatively by images showing exceptionally thin female models, exposure to fashion imagery has detrimental psychological affects for both men and women across the lifespan.

While comparison with others is an important risk factor for body dissatisfaction, body image is also negatively impacted by socialisation to cultural beauty expectations and gender stereotypes. Despite the successes of the feminist movement and improvement in some aspects of equality for women, traditional gender roles continue to associate femininity with beauty, and masculinity with power. Gender socialisation emphasises women's physical attractiveness as a measure of their social value and perpetuates societal objectification by continuous cultural scrutiny. Moreover, stereotypically feminine traits such as dependence and passivity engender low self-esteem and the need to seek approval from others. This can manifest through the pursuit of the 'ideal' body as women, and increasingly men, develop a self-critical orientation towards their physical appearance that results in negative body esteem.

The development of a negative body image can start in early childhood when the perceptions of one's body's attractiveness, health and acceptability are established through feedback from friends, family and peers. Children as young as 4 years old make preferential choices for slimmer over plumper figures, and 6-year-old children prefer 'normal' weight rather than overweight friends. Interestingly, even at this age, boys are more accepting of overweight children. This could be due to parental influence and comments on their children's appearance and eating patterns, with more pressure put on girls than boys to be slim. In addition, prejudice against overweight individuals is perpetuated through media including children's cartoons, books and video games, which portray overweight characters as unattractive, unintelligent and antisocial. In addition, toys promote unrealistic body ideals and cultivate gendered pursuits. Psychologists have found that girls aged 5 to 8 years reported a lower body esteem and increased body size dissatisfaction after exposure to images of Barbie dolls. Adolescent girls have been found to be more vulnerable to media influences and to engage in more social appearance comparison than adolescent boys. However, recent research suggests males are increasingly affected by body ideals and, like women, are resorting to supplements and diets to change their body shape. The difference is that women tend to want to lose fat to be slimmer, and men want to lose fat so their muscles appear more defined.

A 2017 report from the Children's Society UK shows that children are happiest with their relationships with family and least happy with school and their appearance.[4] As usual, boys were happier with their appearance than girls, but the difference has narrowed since previous surveys. Girls are more satisfied with life in general than boys at an early age, but between the ages of 10 and 15 years, the average happiness with life as a whole decreases substantially for girls; for boys it remains stable. This could be a result of being bullied about appearance or of the onset of physiological and psychological changes at puberty which result in greater concern with appearance. In addition, evaluations from friends and peers impact the development of self-concept and body image. Dealing with the bodily changes and resulting evaluations make this a tough time for girls especially as they strive to achieve the thin ideal. Although most research on body image has been based on samples of girls and women, increasingly men are also experiencing, or at least reporting, body image issues. The limited research that exists on body image issues in males suggests that cultural shifts in the ways men's bodies are represented are leading them to feel increasingly dissatisfied with their appearance.

Many researchers have found that rates of body image concerns and disordered eating increase rapidly in early adolescence, with over 45% of early adolescent girls reporting body dissatisfaction. The physical changes associated with puberty tend to move young girls further away from the androgynous and extremely slender body ideal promoted by fashion media. In contrast, puberty in boys tends to increase muscularity, moving them closer to the social ideal. Nonetheless, almost a quarter of early adolescent boys also report being dissatisfied with their bodies.

During their college years, males and females experience increasing pressures related to physical appearance, which take their toll on psychological health and ultimately general behaviour. Several correlational studies demonstrate a strong relationship between social comparisons with peers and disordered eating in women at college. However, young college women have been found to compare themselves to the thin ideal media images as frequently as they compare themselves to peers. Indeed, the tendency to make social comparisons is stronger in college women with eating disorder symptoms. Moreover, these women make more negative appraisals of their own bodies when shown pictures of other women's bodies because the influence of physical attractiveness on self-concept has been found to be stronger for women than for men. Despite this, an increasingly large literature demonstrates that pressure from the mass media to conform to the muscular 'ideal' male body negatively affects men's and boys' body satisfaction, body esteem and self-esteem. Over the past decades, the idealised male body has become increasingly muscular as they focus more on their appearance. This can contribute to low body image satisfaction among men.

Research commissioned by the YMCA and Succeed Foundation and conducted by Dr Phillipa Diedrichs at the University of the West of England, found that 80% of men, compared with 75% of women, had anxieties about their body's perceived flaws and imperfections. As a result, some men participated in compulsive exercise, strict diets and other disordered eating to lose weight or achieve a more toned physique. Almost one quarter of the men surveyed said that their appearance had deterred them from going to the gym. Respondents blamed the media and celebrities for unhelpfully reinforcing unrealistic ideals of physical perfection. Recent research found that American men are just as likely as women to be dissatisfied with their bodies,[5] that adolescent boys who are dissatisfied with their body shape are more likely than girls to be self-critical and distressed,[6] and that men feel worse about their bodies after playing video games with muscular characters.[7]

Most people feel unhappy about the way they look for short periods of time at some point in their life. However, for those individuals with dysmorphia, these thoughts persist and, despite reassurances from others about their appearance, are so distressing they impact on daily life. Body dysmorphic disorder is described as a mental health problem. Dysmorphia is an anxiety disorder that causes a person to have an obsessive preoccupation with and distorted view of how they look, along with pervasive, intrusive thoughts that some aspect of their appearance is severely flawed and warrants exceptional measures to hide or fix it. Preoccupation with weight and shape has been found to lead to psychological distress and eating disorders in girls, whereas it leads to dietary restraint and binge-eating in boys. Across the lifespan, males and females tend to report different strategies for managing their body image. Females are more likely to engage in upward social comparisons regarding their appearance, perceiving other women to be more attractive, whereas men are more likely to make downward social comparisons, which enhances their self-esteem.

Body dysmorphic disorder typically starts during adolescence but generally remains undiagnosed. Because it is difficult to diagnose, only 2.4% of men and women are known to be affected. However, it can impair quality of life at school, at work and in social interactions, and it can increase the risk of eating disorders, self-harm and attempted suicide as well as leading to an increased interest in cosmetic surgery. Clearly, not every case of negative body satisfaction would be categorised as a mental health problem, but the increasing prevalence of body dissatisfaction across genders and the age span is alarming, not least because body dissatisfaction has been found to predict disordered eating; depressive symptoms; low self-esteem; weight gain and reduced physical activity or, conversely, over-exercising; and, of course, demand for cosmetic interventions.

BEAUTY AND COSMETIC INTERVENTIONS

The role of beauty or physical attractiveness is socially and culturally determined and highly valued in fashion and in society. When women do not conform to the current ideal of beauty, they can feel alienated. An individual perceived as physically attractive is subconsciously imbued with a host of other positive qualities such as being warmer, stronger, more poised, and more sociable, dominant, sexually warm, mentally healthy, intelligent and socially skilled than unattractive people. These biases towards attractive people begin in childhood and persevere into adulthood. Consequently, beautiful adults fare better in social spheres despite the lack of evidence to support the existence of attractiveness-related qualities. One problem is that, in reality, highly attractive people are rare, but they are over-represented in fashion, the media and entertainment, where they are portrayed as more desirable, credible and inspirational. This misrepresentation perpetuates the notion that 'what is beautiful is good' because it reinforces the values, norms and ideals of fashion and beauty via fashion and other imagery. The notion that what is beautiful is good combined with the normalised perfect ideal can lead individuals to seek ways to dramatically change their appearance, for example, through cosmetic interventions.

Increasing numbers of younger women and men are electing to have cosmetic surgery, but the psychological impact of these interventions is not fully known as many are conducted by unregistered practitioners who, until recently, have practiced without the requirement for regulation. In a survey of 322 university students, body appreciation, media influence and internalisation of media messages as well as media coverage of cosmetic procedures and weight status were found to be the most significant predictors of considering cosmetic surgery among female undergraduates.[8] A review of 37 relevant studies on psychological and psychosocial outcomes for individuals undergoing cosmetic surgery found that patients were generally satisfied with the outcome, but some, mainly young males and patients with body dysmorphic disorder, were dissatisfied.[9] This is considered a result of unrealistic expectations, previous experience of unsatisfactory cosmetic surgery, minimal deformity, motivation based on relationship issues, and a history of a range of psychological issues.

Worryingly, the private sector for cosmetic interventions remains largely unregulated, and many procedures are performed by unqualified practitioners conducting work on vulnerable individuals. The impact of such practice is yet to be fully realised, but given the association between body image concerns, the internalisation of the thin ideal, and increased interest in undergoing cosmetic surgery, it is a cause for serious concern. A 2016 report by the American Society for Aesthetic Plastic Surgery shows that the total spent on surgical and nonsurgical cosmetic procedures rose from just over US$1.5 million in 1997 to more than US$13.6 million in 2016. Surgical procedures, 56% of the total expenditures in 2016, had increased 3.5% from 2015. The surgical procedures that increased most include fat transfer to the breast (up 41%, with more than 25,000 procedures performed), labiaplasty (up 23%), buttock lift (up 21%), fat transfer to the face (up 17%) and breast implant removal (up 13%). Nonsurgical procedures include photo rejuvenation (up 36%, 650,000 procedures performed), hyaluronic acid, which aims to keep the skin moisturised (up 16%), laser tattoo removal (up 13%), nonsurgical skin tightening (up 12%) and botulinum toxin to reduce or remove the appearance of wrinkles (up 8%).[10]

The top five surgical procedures for women in 2016 were liposuction (369,323 procedures), breast augmentation (310,444 procedures), tummy tuck (173,536 procedures), breast lift (161,412 procedures) and eyelid surgery (145,858 procedures). For men, the top five surgical procedures in 2016 were liposuction (45,012 procedures), breast reduction (31,368 procedures), eyelid surgery (28,025 procedures), nose surgery (26,205 procedures) and facelift (13,702 procedures). Chemical peels, in addition to Botox, hyaluronic acid, hair removal and photo rejuvenation, were the most popular nonsurgical procedures for men. Demand for surgical procedures also varies across the age span. Those in the 35–50 age bracket accounted for 39.3% of the total procedures, whereas those 18 years and under accounted for 1.5% of the total.[11]

In the UK, more than 51,000 people opted for cosmetic surgery in 2015. This represents a 12.6% increase in invasive cosmetic procedures. A report by the British Association of Aesthetic and Plastic Surgeons expressed concern that plastic surgery could become a commodity. Women accounted for 91% of cosmetic procedures in the UK. While surgery on men in the UK appears to be relatively uncommon compared to cosmetic interventions for men in the USA, the number of men undergoing cosmetic procedures in the UK has doubled over the past 10 years as a result of changes in men's fashion styles and a move away from the 'hyper-masculine' look to a more slimline appearance. The interventions in order of popularity in the UK are breast augmentation (up 12% from 2014), eyelid surgery (up 12%), face/neck lift (up 16%), breast reduction (up 13%), liposuction (up 20%), rhinoplasty (up 14%), fat transfer (up 3%), abdominoplasty (up 8%) and brow lift (up 7%).[12]

A comprehensive 2017 report by the Nuffield Council on Bioethics highlights some of the many and complex issues involved in the supply and demand for cosmetic interventions. The report considers many factors that may influence people's decisions to seek invasive non-reconstructive cosmetic procedures to enhance or 'normalise' their appearance. Among other factors, it discusses the impact on wider society of the growing use of cosmetic procedures, and the sociocultural contexts that play a role in stimulating demand for those procedures. Evidence used in the report demonstrates that rising levels of 'body dissatisfaction' are associated with increased use of social media, celebrity culture, economic and social trends and a culture that values youthfulness.[13]

These influences are reinforced by advertising and marketing through the message that beauty is positively correlated with happiness and success. As a result, and with so much at their fingertips, women sense that they have a duty to make the best of themselves in all things including appearance. After discussing the evidence, the report makes many recommendations, including the need for improved ethical practice on both the demand and supply sides. On the demand side, the report recommends action from the Advertising Standards Authority, social media companies, Ofcom, the Equality and Human Rights Commission, the Department for Education and app stores. With regard to the supply of cosmetic interventions, the report urges the Royal College of Surgeons to consider how best to continue taking a leadership role in supporting high standards in cosmetic surgery. It argues that children and young people under the age of 18 should not be able to access invasive cosmetic procedures other than in the context of multidisciplinary health care. Major providers of cosmetic procedures should collaborate to fund the independent development of high-quality information for users and to develop a code of best practices for the provision of cosmetic procedures. Lastly, the Royal College of Surgeons, the General Medical Council, the major providers of cosmetic surgery, and professional bodies representing surgeons in the cosmetic sector should work together to ensure that all surgeons undertaking cosmetic surgery are certified to do so and can access necessary training.

Certain psychopathological symptoms have been found to predict interest in cosmetic surgery, which suggests that counselling prior to surgery and monitoring afterwards would be helpful. In a 2007 meta-analysis by Frederick et al., surveys with 25,714 men and 26,963 women across the lifespan were compared.[14] The findings showed twice as many women as men were interested in cosmetic surgery. Distorted eating behaviour was a significant positive predictor of interest in plastic surgery. Sadly, researchers have reported an increased risk of suicide among women with breast implants, which could potentially be predicted based on the characteristics of these women. They found that education and quality of parental relationships were predictors of interest in cosmetic surgery. Other research shows that knowing someone who has undergone cosmetic surgery increases interest in having surgery oneself, as does being teased about one's physical appearance in childhood or adolescence. Reading fashion blogs is associated with greater internalisation of the thin ideal and a greater tendency to consider cosmetic surgery in adolescent girls. While older women experience similar levels of body dissatisfaction to younger women, their body appreciation increases slightly with age despite today's cultural pressures for eternal youthfulness.

Nevertheless, when ageing is portrayed as a disease which must be feared and fought at all costs, and older women are sold the illusion that anti-ageing products will provide the solution they need to combat the natural signs of ageing, it is not surprising that some individuals in this population are attracted towards cosmetic interventions. Overwhelming evidence supports the claim that exposure to media imagery of the 'ideal equals youthful' body and face predicts attitudes towards and consideration of cosmetic surgery, particularly in middle-aged women. Perceptions of the ageing body as unattractive and undesirable may also be related to the greater interest in surgical and nonsurgical interventions among middle-aged and elderly women. Clearly, the cultural ambivalence towards beauty is echoed by that towards ageing. While the male gaze objectifies women, its withdrawal renders them invisible. For women, the loss of beauty and youthfulness, which in contemporary culture are considered synonymous, can lead to a loss of self-definition. This is supported by findings from a qualitative study with a sample of 21 women over the age of 60 who claimed they wanted to "look good" rather than "young, younger, or good for their age".[15]

Ironically, the pressure on women to retain their youthfulness can result in the risk of ridicule by society. On the one hand, both cosmetics and the development of cosmetic interventions have provided women with the potential to appear youthful; on the other, they face society's disapproval for their lack of dignity if they are seen to resort to these methods. However, it is possible for women to feel good about their body in middle age if they have high levels of support and their bodies are accepted by others. In a review of the role of media and peer influences in Australian women's attitudes towards cosmetic surgery, Tiggeman found such women had lower levels of self-objectification and greater appreciation of their own bodies, their health and their functionality and were more accepting of their body imperfections.[16]

Women, and increasingly men, are targeted by advertisers and marketers to purchase products that promise youthful perfection. The global cosmetics industry continues to grow; its value in 2015 was US$210 billion, and the largest sector is anti-ageing products. Young consumers are persuaded by ageist propaganda against the natural signs of ageing that generates biased perceptions of the impossible horror of getting older and inherent ageism. The rate of growth of the anti-ageing market is evidence of its successful influence. The anti-ageing market is projected to be worth US$191.7 billion by 2019. In an extension of the study described previously in which women stated they wanted to look good, not younger, a survey was conducted with more than 500 women aged 45 to 83 years to investigate their perceptions of advertising's effect on their self-esteem.[17] They claimed that a more accurate and representative portrayal in advertising would make them feel better about themselves, more accepting of their changing bodies, more confident, less invisible and more valued by companies and by society as a whole. Older women reportedly have spending power and might be more likely to spend on fashion items if designers, advertisers and marketers considered them as fashion consumers. However, this may not always be the case: the next generation of older adults is likely to have less spending power but more awareness of environmental issues. They will be looking for an ethical and sustainable fashion industry and are likely to vote for this with their wallets.

The pressures for individuals, particularly women, to focus on appearance are in part due to the perceived, and sometimes actual, life benefits available to those considered attractive or beautiful. For example, obese women fare worse than obese men in terms of social mobility and have lower educational and economic attainment, not least because they are less likely to be accepted for further or higher education. As a result, obese women can face job discrimination and hostile work environments, as well as having fewer dating experiences and marriage opportunities.

As discussed, the concept of 'beauty' in the modern world is problematic for many reasons. Fast fixes from cosmetic interventions tempt individuals to change their appearance so that they conform to the stereotype of what is currently considered beautiful. As a result, natural faces and bodies are seen as flawed with abnormalities that can be corrected by cosmetic procedures. "The beautiful woman of the twenty-first century is sculpted surgically from top to bottom, generically neutral, all irregularities regularized, all particularities expunged. She is thus nondisabled, deracialized, and de-ethnicized."[18]

This 'ideal' is portrayed across media including television and film. 'Good' characters are typically portrayed as 'flawless' while 'bad' characters are shown with appearance-related 'imperfections'. This stereotype is damaging for everyone, but particularly for the relatively large population who have a body or facial difference or disfigurement. The UK charity Changing Faces, which helps people who have a disfigurement find a way to live the life they want and campaigns to challenge prejudice and promote respect for differences, published the *Disfigurement in the UK* report on 26 May 2017, Face Equality Day.[19] The report states that at least 1.3 million children, young people and adults in the UK are estimated to have significant disfigurements, including 569,000 with facial disfigurements. Because their disfigurement attracts intrusive attention and the stigma our culture associates with disfigurement, they report feeling self-conscious, isolated and friendless; being teased, ridiculed and stared at in public; and experiencing low expectations in school, problems with employment and stereotyping in the media because of the way they look. For example, in the recent film *Wonder Woman*, the evil Dr Poison had a scarred face. This depiction can socialise individuals to see facial difference as negative and lead to fear of those whose face is different. I am unaware of any fashion campaign or imagery that uses models with a facial difference; hence, this population is excluded. By using the word *disfigure*, Changing Faces means any condition, mark or scar that affects the appearance of a person's face, hands or body. Disfigurement can be present from birth or be acquired during life and can affect anyone from any social or demographic group and at any time.

> Because the face is at the centre of every human being's self-image and the social canvas on which they portray and share their personality and signal their moods and intentions, facial disfigurement can greatly affect a person's self-worth and how others perceive and behave towards them.[20]

Prior to the development of the internet and social media, individuals were less exposed to fashion imagery. Wolf maintains that before the onslaught of visual imagery, physical attraction mattered, but "'beauty' as we understand it, was not, for ordinary women, a serious issue".[21] Taking a feminist stance, she asserts that since the Industrial Revolution, middle-class Western women have been controlled by the 'beauty myth', which promotes and perpetuates ideals and stereotypes. Wolf argues that this myth exploits female guilt and apprehension about their own liberation and provides opportunities for exploitation by marketers. Consequently, women buy into the myth, escalating the beauty industries into one of the most influential global markets.

THE INFLUENCE OF SOCIAL MEDIA ON FASHION CONSUMERS' BODY IMAGE

The human need for social connection is well-established, as are the benefits that people derive from such connections. In the last decade, social networking sites, defined as web-based services that allow internet users to construct a public or semi-public profile, distribute personal content about the self, interact with other individuals and acquire information, have become a major communication tool. Social media is changing the way we communicate. It includes blogs, forums, business networks, photo-sharing platforms, social gaming, microblogs, chat apps and, last but not least, social networks. Social networking sites are becoming the most influential medium for the promotion and distribution of fashion ideas and ideals. Social networking is expected to have 2.95 billion users by 2020. This represents around a third of Earth's entire population. One fifth of these users will be from China, and approximately one in nine from India. In 2016, 78% of the US population had a social networking profile.[22]

According to a report on statistica.com dated August 2017, approximately 2 billion internet users use social networks. Facebook has 2.05 billion monthly active users; Instagram has over 700 million monthly active accounts; and Tumblr has more than 357 million active blog users. The leading social networks are usually available in multiple languages, enabling users to connect across geographical, political or economic borders. Facebook and Google+ focus on friends and family exchanges through photo or status sharing and social games, whereas Tumblr and Twitter focus on rapid communication. Social networking sites are constantly present in their users' lives and therefore have a strong social impact.[23] Many of Facebook's users say they use Facebook as a trustworthy source of news. Instagram, which is almost entirely image-based, is the fastest growing social networking site with 700 million active users, 2 million of whom are mobile users. YouTube has 1.5 billion users, WhatsApp has 1.2 billion users, and Twitter has 328,000 users. These figures are rapidly increasing. While Instagram is used mainly for uploading and editing images, it is also a powerful marketing tool for the fashion and related industries. Having large numbers of followers on Instagram is big business. Currently, Nike has the most followers: 72,000,000, and another 28.1 million follow Nike Football. Victoria's Secret has more than 55 million followers, while Adidas Originals has 20.2 million and Adidas has 14.1 million followers. In the luxury arena, Chanel has 21.6 million followers, Louis Vuitton 17.1 million, Dior 15.5 million, Gucci 1.5 million, Dolce and Gabbana 13.6 million and Prada 12.5 million. Fast fashion, high street brand H&M has 21.1 million, while Zara has 19.5 million.[24]

These days, if a model wishes to be taken seriously, he or she needs to have hundreds of thousands of Instagram followers. Kendall Jenner, Cara Delavigne, Karlie Kloss and Joan Smalls all have millions of followers. American *Vogue* labelled these models as "Instagirls" on its September 2014 cover.[25] Models are now considered much more than the face or body of a campaign; they are seen as 'brand ambassadors' sharing and promoting their brands via their personal channels. Interestingly, models can demand a fee for their services, which is directly related to the number of followers they have. The reasoning behind this is that the number of followers equals media space, which would be expensive in traditional approaches. Instagram has been described as an efficient method for photographers and talent scouts to find potential models. This perceived democratisation could be one reason young women and men spend so long 'perfecting' the images they upload. It instils a sense of sharing or collaboration as well as opportunity. This democratisation of fashion has been seized by fashion bloggers who have become the go-to fashion influencers. Once more, the greater the number of followers a blogger has, the more she or he is in demand by brands.

Word-of-mouth is now considered to be a more powerful influence and a more valuable tool than planned communication from marketing organisations. For example, UK blogger Camille Charrière, who has almost half a million Instagram followers, typically aged 25 to 35 and living in London, New York or Paris, claims that showing fashion on the street is more appealing to consumers than fashion magazines' glamorous shoots.[26] These days, a blogger's number and composition of followers equates with the blogger's worth. These influencers are paid to wear glamorous clothes, attend fashion events and post images of doing so on their Instagram feeds. The more followers an influencer has, the more they can charge for posting. However, some brands are more influenced by the fit of a blogger's image with their brand's image than by their number of followers. Chiara Ferragni, also known as the Blonde Salad, is the world's most popular fashion blogger with 7.7 million followers.[27] She used this to build her own successful fashion business.

Whereas entry into the fashion industry used to be reserved for the privileged, today's technology means that anyone has a chance of making a fortune and living the glamorous life portrayed by those 'ordinary' people they follow. Users of social networking sites can learn how to apply make-up, follow fashion influencers and selectively upload content onto their profiles that best represents their ideal self-views. A review of the beneficial and harmful effects of online communication and social media usage among young people found that these technologies increased self-esteem, perceived social support, social capital, safe identity experimentation and opportunity for self-disclosure, but they also increased exposure to harm, social isolation, depression and cyber-bullying.[28]

Considering that the majority of social media sites are image-based, it becomes apparent that social comparison with regard to appearance could be a serious issue for its users' mental health and wellbeing. As mentioned previously, more than 1.3 million individuals in the UK alone have a disfigurement, and of these more than half a million are facial. The *Disfigurement in the UK* report found that that 96% of respondents to a survey by the UK's face equality charity, Changing Faces, had seen posts and memes on social media which mocked disfigurement. Of those who had reported such a post to a social media company, none had had their complaint upheld. In addition, respondents had experienced high levels of abuse and trolling, yet social media websites seem unwilling to tackle the problem and provide help and support. As a result, Changing Faces is asking the Secretary of State to facilitate a round-table meeting with ministers and representatives of social media companies to address their responsibility to keep their users safe.[29] A more in-depth discussion on the topic of facial appearance is beyond the scope of this book, but for interested readers, please see the suggestions for further reading at the end of the book.

Evidence shows that upward social comparison underlies the deleterious relationship between Facebook use and wellbeing, which results in negative changes in self-esteem, body satisfaction and mental health. Frequent Facebook users perceived that other users were happier and more successful than they were, and this was amplified when they did not know the other users well offline. In a focus group study designed to explore participants' emotional experiences with Facebook, users reported that being exposed to others' information often generated feelings of being tethered to Facebook because it was so accessible and because they felt pressured by friends, relatives and romantic partners to engage in relationship maintenance on the site. As a result, they had a sense of 'missing out' if they did not check the site regularly. This emotional response has been termed FOMO, a fear of missing out. This fear created additional pressures and sometimes led to unhealthy behaviours, such as monitoring certain people's online activities and engaging in regular social comparison.

One might imagine that discussing one's insecurities about one's appearance with friends and family would be cathartic. However, research has found that complaining to friends and family about one's appearance, body size, weight and fear of becoming fat can negatively impact feelings about the self.[30] Nevertheless, women of all ages and body sizes feel pressure to be self-critical about their bodies.[31] More women than men report exposure to 'fat talk' and greater pressure to engage in it.[32] Research has found that men's body talk is related to weight and muscularity.[33] When body talk is about weight, it results in upper body dissatisfaction, symptoms of muscle dysmorphia, and disordered eating attitudes and behaviours. When body talk is about muscularity, it is associated with dissatisfaction with the upper body, a strong drive for muscularity, symptoms of muscle dysmorphia, and investment in appearance. However, men engage in positive as well as negative body talk, whereas women tend to engage in negative body talk only. In a sample of 203 young adult women, negative body talk was related to body dissatisfaction, poor self-esteem, stronger investment in appearance, distorted thoughts about the body, disordered eating behaviour and depression.[34] Positive body talk was related to fewer cognitive distortions of the body, high body satisfaction, high self-esteem and friendship quality.

The current ubiquity of visual imagery has contributed to an appearance-oriented culture, which supports a 'pervasive objectification of women'. Modern Western culture encourages women to develop observers' views of their bodies; much of this is generated through media which depicts ideals for both male and female bodies: men are portrayed as large and muscular, whereas women are portrayed as thin and beautiful. As discussed, the media tend to sexually objectify women's bodies more than men's bodies. Individuals experience self-discrepancy and shame when their comparisons with cultural ideals do not relate well. Often, people who are ashamed feel a sense of exposure and a heightened concern with others' opinions.

OBJECTIFICATION

Objectification is a pervasive form of sexual oppression in which the individual is viewed as a body for use or consumption by others. Objectification theory predicts that women's continual comparison with the media's body ideals results in body shame.[35] It is an integrative framework for understanding how women's socialisation and experiences of sexual objectification are translated into mental health problems. In current culture, the female body is frequently construed as an object to be looked at and sexually gazed upon. The most subtle way that objectification is enacted is through the gaze, visual inspection of the body. This occurs when a woman's body is perceived as separated from her as a person and regarded as representative of her. In this sense, objectified women are treated as bodies that exist for the use and pleasure of others, which results in persistent body surveillance or monitoring.

Objectification theory demonstrates how objectification takes place in interpersonal and social encounters and via visual media where women find themselves stared at more than men and feel 'looked at' more. Gazing is often accompanied by sexually evaluative, and often derogatory, commentary. In visual media, notwithstanding the obviously problematic issues of the pornography industry, the sexually objectifying gaze also occurs in mainstream films, advertisements, visual arts, television, music videos, magazines, sports photography and fashion. The most profound psychological effect of objectifying, according to objectification theory's creators, Fredrickson and Roberts, is that it can lead females to treat themselves as objects to be looked at and evaluated.[36]

Women who score high on self-objectification report the most disordered eating and higher levels of body dissatisfaction regardless of their reaction to appearance comments, whereas women scoring low on self-objectification report different levels of body dissatisfaction depending on their reaction to such comments. As objectification can lead to greater body monitoring, it can exacerbate symptoms of eating disorders. In a 2004 study, college women with high levels of body dissatisfaction who constantly monitored their bodies were found to be more likely to spend longer being aware of their dissatisfaction. The author argued that during their college years, women may be more vulnerable to self-objectification and its negative effects, which include increased appearance anxiety, fewer peak motivational states, diminished awareness of internal bodily states, increased anxiety about physical safety, and increased body shame.[37] How women internalise objectification influences their emotional and cognitive behaviour. For example, researchers found that wearing a swimsuit affected women's, but not men's, performance on a maths test.[38] Other studies have asked women to see themselves wearing a swimsuit or a sweater in front of a full-length mirror. They report that trying on a swimsuit increased self-consciousness and body shame and lowered self-esteem, whereas the sweater did not. Importantly, those who wore the swimsuit continued to think about their body even when they had changed back into their own clothes.[39] In another study gay and heterosexual male participants were asked to try on either Speedos or a turtleneck sweater and then sample and evaluate a snack.[40] The findings showed that gay participants who had tried on Speedos ate significantly less of the snack than heterosexual men in the Speedo condition, and significantly less than gay men in the sweater condition.

Generally, women report higher levels of appearance anxiety than men, which is evidenced by the millions of dollars they spend each year on cosmetics, surgery and weight reduction programs in an attempt to achieve the ideal. Women with higher appearance anxiety have low self-esteem, high public self-consciousness and high audience and test anxiety. This sort of anxiety is considered to be a consequence of self-objectification in a culture which emphasises the importance of appearance for women far more than for men. Body shame, appearance anxiety and disgust that results from self-objectification can also result in decreased sexual interest or negative attitudes towards sex. Women who are self-conscious about their body consume cognitive resources monitoring their bodies during sexual situations and as a result find them less enjoyable.

Objectification can be primed merely by objectifying words. A study with 70 male and 90 female undergraduate students investigated the link between sexually objectifying words or messages and the onset of self-objectification.[41] The findings showed that words alone were enough to generate self-objectification even with educated women who were aware of the unreality of media images and were motivated to disregard them. The authors proposed that media literacy education should expose print media as a priming mechanism for objectification to enable women to recognise that they should be cautious when reading objectifying words as well as viewing objectifying pictures.

Although the majority of work on objectification has shown that women fare worse than men, the recent interest in protein powders, muscle enhancers, Viagra and hair loss remedies has negative effects on men's self-concepts. In addition, men may evaluate themselves from observers' perspectives on dimensions unrelated to appearance, such as sexual prowess and financial success.[42] Using more diverse images of women and men in the mass media would help reduce the incidences of self-objectification and the associated negative outcomes as these images would offset the sexually objectified, ultrathin women with more realistic images of women.

SUMMARY

In recent years, the image-based social media platform Instagram has overtaken Facebook in terms of new users. People use Instagram for many reasons, including social interaction, archiving of personal records, self-expression, escapism and looking at the photos of other users. However, when we believe that we do not compare favourably with the people portrayed in social media images, and as they become the prevailing norm, we feel dissatisfied and strive to reduce the discrepancy between our actual and our ideal self. In doing so we may resort to extreme measures including pursuing unhealthy diet and exercise regimes, embarking on sometimes risky cosmetic procedures and even developing eating disorders including anorexia nervosa and bulimia. Although cause and effect cannot be established, researchers have found associations between exposure to fashion and media imagery and body image issues including body dissatisfaction and eating disorders. Despite the common practice of judging girls and women on their appearance and men on their strength, dexterity or intellect, the pressure for the 'ideal' appearance is increasingly being applied across genders. The market for anti-ageing creams, gravity-defying potions and surgical and nonsurgical cosmetic interventions feeds an appearance-obsessed society which judges individuals by how well they measure up to the media stereotype of youthful perfection. The obsession with appearance is worrying particularly when it manifests as objectification. When the current obsession with appearance is combined with the escalating demand for cosmetic interventions as a quick fix for appearance dissatisfaction, it becomes a serious cause for concern.

4

FASHION, SELF AND IDENTITY

OVERVIEW

Self and identity are of interest in many disciplines, including fashion theory, cultural theory, philosophy, anthropology, sociology and psychology. In history, clothing was a means of stratifying people according to class, occupation, region and so on, but more recently subcultures. Subcultures are often defined by their clothing, which simultaneously separates and unites groups across different genres such as music and politics. We cannot separate clothing from the self and identity because what we wear is an outward display of our self and our identity.

SELF AND IDENTITY

Despite differing definitions, there is some agreement that 'self' refers to a process of reflection and reflexivity that develops in social interaction as a result of socialisation. Socialisation is the vehicle through which we become socially adjusted to the standards of our community and society. It is the process of acquiring and propagating norms, customs, values and ideologies that enable individuals to function appropriately throughout the lifespan within their societies. Girls are often socialised to value the qualities that align them to others, whereas boys are taught to value the qualities that distinguish and differentiate them from others. As these values extend through the lifespan, women tend to develop more interdependent selves and relate their self-esteem to the quality of their relationships, whereas men tend to develop more independent selves associated with their self-esteem. The self is socially constructed, and the socialisation process is never complete. Although we develop our self-concept through socialisation, we continually assess it by measuring it against societal and cultural norms and the feedback we receive from others.

The self comprises multifaceted, interrelated components including self-awareness, self-concept, self-esteem, self-knowledge and self-perception and is integral in motivation, cognition, affect and social identity. Identity is considered to develop from infancy throughout the lifespan as a result of factors regarded as possessions.

According to William James, who is often considered the founding father of psychology, the self comprises multiple components including

> all that the person can call his or her own, not only his body and his psychic powers, but his clothes and his house, his wife and children, his ancestors and friends, his reputation and works, his lands and horses, and yacht and bank-account.[1]

Consequently, we feel and act about certain belongings in a similar way to how we feel and act about ourselves, but not always. We find it difficult to separate what we call 'Me' from what we call 'Mine' because they are a continuum.

Clothing is part of our identity, and fashion provides an obvious means for presenting the self in the most favourable way. Many factors influence how a person dresses including the amount of money they have to spend on clothing, their body shape and the availability of items in fashion stores that fit them, the amount of time they have to shop and their degree of self-awareness. In addition, sometimes we care more about what we are wearing than others, and sometimes we are restricted in our clothing by social, cultural and occupational norms and rules. Many reasons have been given for following fashion, including for enhancement of one's best feature, for modesty and for status and in-group belonging and out-group differentiation. In this sense, clothing is a way of satisfying our needs, and when these are met, we can use it to articulate our identity.

Maslow's 1943 hierarchy of needs model is a popular motivation theory in social science and has been used to explain a wealth of behaviours as well as how clothing satisfies human needs.[2] For example, the lowest physiological and safety needs of the hierarchy can be met by clothing as it comforts and protects the wearer. The next layers of the hierarchy – love, belonging and self-esteem – can be satisfied when we use our clothing to enhance or enact our social identity, and while some researchers claim that self-actualisation can be achieved through individualistic or creative dress that does not harm the environment, this might be an exaggeration of the power of fashion. For Maslow, self-actualisation was achieved by only a few as a result of giving back, rather than just doing no harm. In fact, in Maslow's later extension of the five-layer model, he added the layer of Transcendence and stated that actualisation is achieved by giving oneself spiritually or altruistically to something larger than oneself. In this sense,

> Transcendence refers to the very highest and most inclusive or holistic levels of human consciousness, behaving and relating, as ends rather than means, to oneself, to significant others, to human beings in general, to other species, to nature, and to the cosmos.[3]

It remains to be seen if this can be achieved through fashion.

A 1963 study with 300 college women showed correlations between (i) behaviour related to the use of clothing as a status symbol and the need for self-esteem, and (ii) the use of clothing to enhance personal appearance.[4] Self-enhancement and impression management are motivating factors in maintaining positive self-esteem.

Most individuals seek positive feedback and have favourable self-views, which shape their assumptions about how others view them. Because we have favourable self-views and seek positive feedback, we choose clothing that conveys social status, adopt social roles that communicate self-perceptions, and communicate in a manner that generates self-confirming feedback. Individuals who are concerned about their appearance and the impression they make on others tend to believe clothes can influence their mood, make an effort to be fashionable and believe their impressions of others are influenced by what the others are wearing. Such people are likely to be high self-monitors, to be more interested and involved in clothing, to be more fashionable while conforming to social norms and to use clothing as a form of relieving social anxiety. High self-monitors are more positive towards adverts which emphasise image rather than product quality, and more willing to pay more for clothing than low self-monitors. Comments and evaluations from others provide self-knowledge and can influence self-concept, self-identity and self-esteem. Typically, individuals attempt to enhance their self-esteem by making upward or downward comparisons, and they misinterpret, distort and ignore disconfirming information. Fashion has an important role to play in this respect. Many individuals make upward comparisons to the unattainable 'ideal', the norm promoted in the media by the fashion industries, and as a result develop negative emotions about their own appearance which can lead to extreme exercise programmes, weight control, cosmetic interventions or even surgery.

Clothing and appearance play an important role in the development, maintenance and modification of the self and are part of the way we view and think about ourselves. Individuals who are depressed have been found to distort their self-image negatively, to report low self-esteem and lower body satisfaction and to view themselves as less attractive than non-depressed people. Self-esteem is the evaluative component of self-concept or self-image, the mental depiction of our physical and psychological characteristics based on personal experiences and internalised judgements of or comparisons to others and our role in society. People with high self-esteem view their self as containing positive traits and are more likely to be optimistic, confident and ambitious and to take risks. They worry less about what others think of them than those with low self-esteem, who tend to be pessimistic, with few or no self-perceived positive traits. The norms of the groups we identify with socially and emotionally define our behaviour and influence our self-esteem. When there's a mismatch between our self-image and our ideal self, our self-esteem suffers.

Self-esteem is not fixed and can change as a factor of context. Researchers seated job applicants next to either an applicant dressed formally in a suit, carrying a briefcase containing a slide rule and books, or another dressed casually in a T-shirt and jeans, reading a sex novel.[5] As predicted by social comparison theory, the self-esteem of the applicants seated next to the formally dressed candidate decreased significantly, and the self-esteem of the applicants seated next to the casually dressed candidate increased significantly. In the same study, as predicted by social identity theory, similarity between the applicant and the clothing style of the person they were seated next to enhanced self-esteem, while dissimilarity reduced it.

THEORIES OF SELF

Self-perception theory is concerned with attitude formation.[6] It suggests that any variable, including appearance, that affects our impressions of others may also affect our impressions of self. Although we are able to introspect and examine our own conscious feelings and thoughts to gather information about our self, many of our actions are unconscious, and these, by definition, are not available for introspection. In addition, we imagine how others see and judge us so that we develop a favourable response. We make social comparisons with those around us, particularly those we consider to be in the same category. Self-perception theory was used to investigate whether wearing a specific item of dress would influence people's ratings of their own skills and abilities. Researchers asked participants to rate themselves when wearing or not wearing glasses and to complete a hidden figures test.[7] Although there were no significant differences in their performance on the test, the participants' ratings of their competence and intelligence were higher when wearing glasses than when not. Research on self-perception has found that participants would feel more competent and responsible if they wore appropriate rather than inappropriate work clothing.[8] Others have found that participants saw themselves as most authoritative, trustworthy, productive and competent when wearing formal business attire, but as friendliest when wearing casual or business casual attire.[9] Guy and Banim (2000) investigated women's relationships to their clothing via a personal account, clothing diary and wardrobe interview.[10] They identified three perspectives of self relative to clothing: "the woman I want to be", "the woman I fear I could be" and "the woman I am most of the time".[11]

As we develop across the lifespan, our cognitive structures, including our perceptual processes, become more able to create a unified social world. We organise our thoughts and simplify our perceptions accordingly and make assumptions about others' characters and abilities based solely on their appearance. Social learning theory outlines how behaviour is learnt by observing others such as parents, family members, friends and teachers as well as characters in the media and imitating their behaviour.[12] As children interact with others, they receive feedback on their behaviour. Therefore, if a child imitates a behaviour and is subsequently rewarded for it, he or she will continue that behaviour, which becomes internalised as values, beliefs and attitudes. These processes continue into adulthood and are the basis of group dynamics. We choose to identify with those whom we perceive as like-minded, who look similar to ourselves, who have a similar level of attractiveness and who dress similarly. Although we want to belong, we also want to feel unique, to differentiate ourselves from others. The opposing processes of identification, our psychological need to belong, and differentiation, the need to feel unique, are implicated in our sense of self. This dichotomy has been described as the most important driver for fashion change.

As social perceivers, we learn about others by observing and interpreting their physical appearance and communication, including gestures, posture, facial expressions and movement. From our observations, we attribute their behaviour to their disposition or personality and then seek to confirm this by means of our various biases, shaped by our motivations, emotions, expectations, knowledge and beliefs about the social world. To do this efficiently, we categorise objects, including people, and evaluate them based on categories that are important to our own self-concepts. This results in effort-free, automatic stereotypical thinking which satisfies our preference for cognitive ease but can lead to inaccurate associations. In stereotyping, we assign individuals to particular social groups which we perceive as similar to them, based on limited information, often appearance. Social psychologists have studied stereotyping from multiple perspectives including race and ethnic identity, sex, social status, body types, physical attractiveness, hair and age. These stereotypes underpin much of the research about what our clothes say about us.

According to social comparison theory, humans are driven to assess their progress and standing in life by seeking standards against which to compare themselves, potentially for perceived self-improvement.[13] We do this through upward social comparison, when we compare ourselves with others whose positive characteristics we consider to be superior, or downward social comparison, when we compare ourselves with inferior others who have negative characteristics. Upward social comparison often leads to feelings of inadequacy, whereas downward comparison often leads to enhanced affect and self-evaluation. In a 1970 study, male participants were asked to complete a self-evaluation questionnaire including items such as "I'm a good person".[14] While they were doing this, a well-groomed or poorly groomed experimenter entered the room. The experimenter's appearance influenced the participants' responses such that the well-groomed experimenter led to more positive self-evaluations than the poorly groomed experimenter. This demonstrates how comparisons affect our self-concept. Social comparison theory predicts that we make comparisons that result in favourable outcomes, with those we perceive as most similar to us. However, recent research has shown that women evaluate their bodies by making appearance-based upward social comparisons to media images and women they perceive to be thinner and more attractive than they are. Although upward comparisons often result in discontentment and dissatisfaction, women make these comparisons regularly, potentially as a result of being evaluated more than men on their physical appearance. Self-discrepancy theory describes how individuals hold differing beliefs about their actual and ideal selves based on particular variables such as weight or attractiveness, which motivate them to try to achieve that ideal.[15] Problems arise when the media sells women the message that they can control their appearance and bodies and, with effort, can comply with cultural standards of thinness. As a result, many women feel they must engage in constant body surveillance while striving for the thin ideal. In doing so they experience a discrepancy between their actual and ideal appearance.

Social identity theory argues that we derive pride and self-esteem from the groups we belong to and that we enhance our self-image through enhancing the status of the group (the in-group) and discriminating against those not in the group (the out-group).[16] Clothing can communicate our group association when it has social identity congruence and is used as a social symbol. Social identities, including youth versus age, male versus female, masculine versus feminine, inclusivity versus elitism, conformity versus rebellion and so on, emerge throughout the lifespan, but individual differences determine how strongly we identify with these categories. We may join groups as a means of self-enhancement or for self-categorisation. Fashion can allow us to stand out as different or fit in as the same. Groups may have a 'uniform' that identifies membership, and our desire to be part of the group will influence the way we dress. Following the latest trends can give us membership in the 'fashionable' group. This presents a dilemma for fashion as it is often portrayed as the desire to look different.

SELF, IDENTITY, FASHION AND INCLUSIVITY

Several researchers emphasise the importance of clothing to the concept of self, arguing that clothing is a medium through which the self is realised. For example, when adolescent girls share clothes, they also share identities. Our relationship with possessions starts from a very early age. Research has found that children at 2 years of age are able to understand the notion of possessing something as if it were part of ourselves. Our possessions can become external repositories for particular events within our lives. Researchers from positive psychology have noted that specific garments hold symbolic meanings of meaningful memories. They concluded that even though an item of clothing was no longer being worn, it was kept as it had transcended its utilitarian function and instead acted as a nostalgic connector to memories.

Fashion provides a visual and readily available vehicle for negotiating self-identity and self-expression whether one is seeking novelty, individualism or belonging through the concepts of in-group and out-group. While fashion appears to some to be superficial, to others fashion has a depth that echoes the depth of human self-awareness.[17] Certainly, its importance to the individual is reflected in the profitability of the fashion industry. Early commentators on fashion, including economist Thorstein Veblen and social psychologist Georg Simmel, focused on the role of fashion in negotiating class in identity, but, recently, 'lifestyles' rather than class have become more influential in identity formation.

Because of socialisation, the behaviour, beliefs and attitudes of males and females vary across the lifespan in relation to clothing. Clothes have been found to be important to adolescent boys and girls, but for different reasons. Adolescent girls tend to be influenced by their friends in their clothing choice, whereas boys are influenced by their own choices. For males, self-concept is enhanced by increased muscle strength, and findings show that boys like to wear clothing that shows off their muscles. However, a 1989 study by Kaiser and Freeman with 30 male and 30 female students found that males related their clothing preferences in terms of personal accomplishments or sentimental events, whereas females related clothing to emotions and feelings experienced when wearing the item.[18] This finding can be explained by socialisation when females are exposed to pressures to be 'pretty' and 'passive'; as a result, women tend to evaluate themselves on attractiveness, and men evaluate themselves on effectiveness. Women report feeling close to their clothing, whereas men relate their clothing to how they feel about themselves. In studies investigating self-schema, researchers found that the more clothes were perceived as like the wearers, the more readily the respondents could identify situations where they would wear them. When the self is considered a process, wearers are concerned about others' responses to their appearance as a result of their clothing. This can have detrimental effects, as predicted by objectification theory, discussed in Chapter 3. While we like to associate ourselves with some groups and disassociate ourselves from others, we are aligned to others as a result of our appearance, gender, age, ethnicity, economic status and so on. However, there is little representation in fashion of diverse populations. Consequently, swathes of the population are ignored, marginalised or misrepresented. It makes sense that using more diverse imagery and being more inclusive in fashion representation could alleviate many of the negative psychological and social outcomes we currently face.

Given that our self-esteem is determined by measurement against the norm, it is not surprising that many groups of the population feel marginalised by fashion. The narrow stereotype of beauty determined and promoted by the fashion and media industries is problematic in many senses, not least in that it does not represent the diverse population which consumes its products. Diversity encompasses acceptance of and respect for difference and uniqueness along the dimensions of race, ethnicity, gender, sexual orientation, socio-economic status, age, physical ability and religious, political or other ideologies. Bodies come in all shapes, sizes, skin tones and abilities, and they adapt across the lifespan to perform ordinary and extraordinary actions.

Although there have been improvements recently, it is still the exception to see fashion imagery portraying a diverse population that goes any way towards accurately representing its audience. For example, it is still rare to see individuals who are from Black and Minority Ethnic (BAME) populations, older people (especially women), disabled individuals or normal-weight and larger people on the catwalk or elsewhere in the fashion media. This is a major issue that could be resolved by the fashion industry for mutual benefit as researchers have found that consumers like to see clothes on people who look like they do so that they can identify with them more readily. However, possibly because of increasing pressure from different sources for diversity in fashion imagery and on the catwalk, it is heart-warming to note that changes are beginning to happen. Unfortunately, the scope of this book limits inclusion of all marginalised groups. This section is intended to highlight the situation of a few and to provoke readers into taking an active stance to change the status quo for the better.

Individuals from BAME populations have a long history of being underrepresented in fashion despite decades of protestations about prejudice which would not be tolerated in other industries. In an analysis of eight popular US fashion magazines in December 2007, researchers found that they contained between 72.94% and 94.08% images of White, non-Latina females, which means that the percentages of Black, Asian, and Latina women in the magazines fell far short of accurately reflecting their proportion of the US population.[19] The researchers argued that this reinforces the 'ideal' as being White (as well as young and thin). Similarly, in a 2007 content analysis of advertisements in five beauty or fashion magazines and five fitness or health magazines, researchers found that 91.28% of the female models depicted in both magazine types were Caucasian.[20]

In attempt to become like the images we see and to acquire social and economic status, people of colour may resort to using dangerous skin-bleaching products and cosmetic surgery. Despite protestations and accusations of racism, entire fashion brands such as Prada have used only White models. An analysis of over 200 London, Paris, Milan and New York womenswear fashion shows between 2001 and 2010 found fewer non-White models than White models, and when non-White models were present, it was often to represent specific ethnic themes or cultural representations.[21] The small but positive change towards greater diversity within the fashion world is evidenced by an increase from 15.3% to 21.8% models of colour used in campaigns from autumn 2015 to spring 2016. They, like everyone, grow older, may be disabled and may not conform to the thin stereotype. We now turn to the matter of ageism, which is rife in everyday life and is perpetuated through fashion.

Unrealistic perceptions of ageing have a negative impact on the psychological and physical health of older people. This is true for both sexes, but for women the problem is exaggerated as sexism exacerbates the implicit bias of ageism. In fashion media and marketing, this prejudice is explicit as older women tend to be excluded and ignored. Despite a significant proportion of readers of fashion magazines being women aged over 35, many studies report under-representation of this population. For example, an analysis of fashion magazines found that 80.72% of the female models were classified as being 21–30 years old,[22] and another found that only 2.68% to 9.02% of images in fashion magazines were of older women. In contrast, the percentage of images of older men in the publications varied between 16.70% and 34.08%.[23] In addition, the narratives of the images in fashion magazines reflected ageism and the preference for young and slender, smooth-skinned and able-bodied individuals.

Although older women tend to be ignored in terms of fashion clothing, they are considered valuable in terms of cosmetics, especially those that promise a youthful appearance. The beauty industry includes cosmetics, skin care, nail and hair care, and scents. One of the most lucrative product lines is concerned with maintaining a youthful appearance while fighting the natural signs of ageing. The media and marketers use fear-based communications to sell so-called anti-ageing products and services, which define the natural process of ageing as a disease that should be fought at any cost. Because negative portrayals of and derogatory messages about ageing are common, older consumers can be influenced to buy anti-ageing products and interventions that would enable them to rejoin society. Older women are shamed into believing they must buy into the pursuit of youth as so many products are available to help them achieve it. This was discussed in the previous chapter on 'beauty'.

Among older women, as in any other population, societal influences and the pressure to conform to the media ideal lead to body dissatisfaction and the drive for thinness and eternal youth. Fashion is not the only medium that misrepresents older females. It is rare to find older women in major roles in UK prime-time television, film or advertising, even in adverts for fashion, clothing and cosmetic products. On the rare occasions they are included, they are portrayed negatively as dependent, needy and feeble, and desexualised; they are digitally altered to disguise their real age and considered inappropriate if they dress in a 'youthful' way. Yet a 2013 study found that only 6% of women over 65 years described themselves as old, almost half complained of ageism, and two thirds were concerned about being seen as a problem by society.[24]

Women can feel conscious about showing their ageing arms because they don't look like the images of arms we constantly see in fashion imagery. Images of models and celebrities who've been digitally altered to show youthful, toned, smooth and firm limbs dominate fashion and media press. Conversely, 'celebrity' magazines take pleasure in shaming those who've been caught unaware showing a more realistic body. Unrealistic imagery in fashion and media can have a detrimental impact on women. Add to this the underrepresentation of older women, and it's not surprising that so few of us dare show our arms.

Adults over 50 account for 47% of UK consumer spending, and people over 65 spend £6.7 billion a year on clothes in Britain.[25] By 2018 one third of the UK population will be over 55 years old, but brands have been slow in seizing this opportunity. However, as with the BAME population, positive changes in terms of greater representation of older women and men in fashion are happening. For example, Lauren Hutton, now aged 73, is modelling Calvin Klein's lingerie; Lyn Slater, a New York university professor aged 63, known on Instagram as the Accidental Icon, is the face of Mango; and H&M's swimwear is being modelled by Gillian McLeod, who is 60 years old. Hardly middle-aged, but still noteworthy in the youth-obsessed world, is British *Vogue* showing Amber Valletta, at 43 years old, as casting agents and brands are beginning to take notice of consumers who want to see clothing on models they can identify with.

Unfortunately, the implicit bias of ageism is so deeply rooted that it can be present without any conscious malice. For example, we sometimes respond to someone's age by saying "You look much younger!", "I wouldn't have thought s/he was that old" or "S/he looks great for her age/that age/50." These exclamations show that we equate looking younger with looking better. The bias is so sub-conscious that when challenged on this, people will say that they do not mean younger is better. Nevertheless, it seems clear that they hadn't intended to insult anyone by telling them they look younger. Until we rid society of this implicit bias, we cannot rid it of ageism.

While we are witnessing slow but positive changes in fashion in relation to the representation of BAME and older individuals, the rep-resentation of disabled individuals remains shockingly poor. Accord-ing to statistics from the charity Scope, there are 13.3 million disabled people in the UK.[26] Despite this potentially influential demographic, individuals with disabilities are typically ignored as fashion consum-ers and in fashion advertising. An early exception to this is Aimee Mullins, an athlete, actor, fashion model and double amputee who was one of *People Magazine*'s 50 Most Beautiful People of 1999. Mul-lins is "an icon of disability pride and equality" who draws attention to the features of her disability.[27] Mullins launched her modelling career with Alexander McQueen in 1999, opening his London show wearing hand-carved wooden prosthetic legs with integral boots. Since then she has been photographed by the world's top fashion photographers, appeared on the cover of international fashion maga-zines and been the face of L'Oréal Paris. Since Mullins' breakthrough, disability has taken a back seat in fashion. However, there are a few noteworthy exceptions. The Diesel spring/summer 2014 advertising campaign featured Jillian Mercado, a wheelchair-using fashion editor and blogger. The fall/winter 2017 New York Fashion Week included an 18-year-old girl with Down syndrome, and a student from Par-sons New York won the Womenswear Designer of the Year award for her collection Seated Design, which sought to empower wheelchair users. Welcome as these innovations are, inclusions of disabled models rarely lead to long-term improvements. It is possible to reflect on these as simply tokenistic gestures. This is the view of Cat Smith, who blogs at Stylishly Impaired and is my doctoral student at London College of Fashion. Smith is investigating the relationship between disability, clothing, fashion and identity for women with mobility impairments. She argues that for these women, as for most other women, clothes are a powerful tool of self-presentation but, in addition, can remove some of the myths that surround disability. Smith emphasises the value of social media as a platform for disabled people to actively represent themselves by promoting their individuality. This contributes to a community where a positive disabled identity exists.

As noted previously, because fashion imagery is omnipresent, it has the potential for shaping public consciousness. Presenting images of disabled fashion models in the media can lead to a cultural shift in the perception of disability and disabled people. Commercial fashion imagery drives desirability through its portrayal of digitally derived 'glamorous perfection'. Its concerns are economic rather than ethical or even aesthetic. However, when disabled fashion models are included in media and on the catwalk, able-bodied people can see disability as 'ordinary' and familiar. In addition, inclusion of disabled fashion models enables people with disabilities to imagine themselves as a part of the ordinary world rather than as "a special class of excluded untouchables and unviewables".[28]

In addition to the marginalised groups discussed already, those who don't conform to the thin ideal are also excluded. According to online data, 67% of women in the USA are size 14 or larger.[29] Sales of women's and girls' colloquially termed *plus-size* clothing rose at double the rate of overall sales to US$21.4 billion in 2016. However, until very recent legislation, the fashion model norm has been very thin. In response to increasing demands for greater diversity in fashion, some brands have publicly stated that they will no longer be using size zero models. Ashley Graham, an American plus-size model, has been featured on the cover of US *Vogue*. Again, a success of social media, Graham has become the role model for hundreds of thousands of women who now can see how a curvy body can be celebrated in fashionable clothing rather than being hidden in dull, utilitarian garb. Nevertheless, there are still limited options for individuals in this population. If they do exist, fashion items in larger sizes are often difficult to find in retail stores and are excluded from the pages of high-fashion publications. As a result, the stigma around being larger is perpetuated by the fashion industry and becomes embedded in the collective consciousness.

The situation faced by marginalised populations has been discussed, but, as is obvious, many of us belong to more than one of these groups. Although our social group may be determined by demographic characteristics such as our place of residence, age, ethnicity, job and income, or by psychosocial factors such as attitudes, beliefs and interests, we can and do fall into several categories. Our social groups are characterised by some degree of social cohesion and identity, often expressed visibly through the clothing worn by members of the group.

SOCIAL GROUPS AND FASHION

We can and do belong to many different groups simultaneously, and those we identify with at a particular time depend on where we are (situationally) at that time. Our in-groups are those we would like to belong to because we admire them, so what we consider as our in-groups may not be where other people see us as belonging. Logos are important to brands as they can make them instantly recognisable. Wearing the logo can mean that the wearer wants to be associated with the brand and the brand personality and image, such as the lifestyle portrayed in the brand's imagery. Being perceived as part of an in-group can mean being perceived (by others as well as oneself) as separate from and superior to other groups (brands). This is why it is important for brands to have distinctive logos and other imagery.

Clothing is significant in human experience, cultures and societies. Clothes reflect and symbolise the traditions, values, emotions and ideologies of the culture in which we are socialised. We derive support and a sense of belongingness from our social groups, which can be defined by their distinctiveness, or *entitativity*.[30] Entitativity is defined as "the perception, either by the group members themselves or by others, that the people together are a group".[31] Strong perceptions of in-group entitativity can help a group's members retain their sense of collective self-esteem and achieve individual psychological needs. Furthermore, perceptions of out-group entitativity can influence pro-social and antisocial behaviours towards them. Factors influencing a group's entitativity are member similarity, interaction and communication, interdependence and structure. But groups can still exist in the absence of these when members simply 'feel' similar to the members of the in-group. This is predicted by social identity theory, which states that feeling good about membership in social groups is important to a positive self-concept. Intentionally or not, our clothing aligns us with a particular social group, our in-group, and dissociates us from other groups, out-groups. Fashion can allow us to stand out as different or fit in as the same.

Fashion subcultures are groups based on certain features of clothing and appearance that make them distinguishable as a subset of the wider culture. The composition and character of a subculture can be defined by demographic factors or by their distinctive appearance. Subcultures aim to be exclusive, and although they may claim that being fashionable is not their mission, they may distinguish themselves from the mainstream by how they dress. Therefore, fashion enables us to achieve social identity, a sense of belonging to the social world. Our desire to be part of the group will influence the way we dress, but we prefer groups whose characteristics we share or aspire to. Following the latest trends can give us membership in the 'fashionable' group. This is a dilemma for fashion as it is often portrayed as the desire to look different.

A youth cult with a definable style in the late 1990s was known as *emo*, short for *emotional*. Emo style originated from the mid-1980s punk rock music movement in Washington, DC. The 1990s music genre known as emo was characterised by more melancholic rock melodies and became popular in the early 2000s. Bands like Jimmy Eat World, Dashboard Confessional and My Chemical Romance attracted a large fan base among teenagers, which of course evolved into an emo fashion movement. Emo fashion was characterised by flat shoes, skinny jeans, black-rimmed glasses and black eye-liner, studded belts, fitted hoodies and vintage band T-shirts. Since then there has been a rise in the popularity of streetwear particularly for men who want to be seen as 'belonging' to something cool, but without an existing subculture they choose clothes and brands that have no cultural link to anything outside of clothes and brands. Of course, this is a statement itself.

Brands such as Supreme cultivate aggressive aloofness, deliberately creating a feeling among their customers that they're 'not cool enough' for the brand. This brand makes its consumers aspire to achieve their coolness rather than achieving it instantly once they have bought into it. For Supreme, wearing their clothes doesn't make you part of their in-group but makes you aspire to be. This manipulative marketing is clever because we enjoy the chase more than the catch. Striving to be as 'cool' as the brand suggests is more exciting for us than really belonging to it. Their strategy encourages us to keep working at it until we make the mark. Desire triggers the release of the 'reward' neurotransmitter, dopamine, which generates motivated behaviour, providing feelings of enjoyment and reinforcement to motivate us to do, or continue doing, certain activities (e.g., in this case, striving to be as cool as the brand suggests). Dopamine is also released when we expect a pleasurable stimulus, which suggests it is involved in desire rather than pleasure. Other research suggests dopamine is important in decision-making by alerting the individual to salient information which may be rewarding or even threatening. Dopamine is a complex neurotransmitter, and readers fascinated by the role it plays in behaviour should consult one of the many texts which exist specifically on this topic.

Clearly an entire fashion world exists beyond the catwalk. A brief overview of a few examples of fashion subcultures based on fashion brands has been included here. However, readers interested in a global perspective are encouraged to read award-winning photographer Daniele Tamagni's book *Fashion Tribes*. The book contains material on Botswana's heavy metal rockers, hipsters in Johannesburg, dandies in the Congo, female wrestlers in Bolivia, 'bling bling' youth in Cuba and punks in Burma. It illustrates how these groups are often marginalised in their own societies and how they retaliate through expressing their personal style.

SUMMARY

This chapter has focused on the role and influence of fashion in relation to the self and identity. It discussed the psychological concepts and theories of self and identity and how these relate to fashion, social groups and subcultures. Many theories of the self and identity exist, and by understanding these, we are more able to predict human behaviour. Our self-concept and self-esteem are reciprocally interrelated, and both are influenced by feedback from others. Fashion media can marginalise many populations, and in doing so it inherently contributes to negative biases about these groups. We try to counter damaging experiences and to enhance our self and identity through self-enhancement tactics and alignment with desirable social groups and subcultures. Fashion is inextricably intertwined with the self, and although clothing allows us to negotiate and define our identity, the degree to which we can do this is complex and dependent on many factors. The following chapter discusses why we wear what we wear and how our clothing can influence behaviour.

5

FASHION CONSUMPTION

OVERVIEW

We cannot ignore the important role of psychology in an understanding of the behaviour of fashion consumers. Psychologists researching the reasons behind our shopping behaviour have found that we shop for many different reasons, including the desire to satisfy a need as well as simply for pleasure. The role of marketers is to increase the sale of goods. Working with an understanding of psychology, marketers identify our needs and show us how we can satisfy them, promising pleasure when we buy a particular product or service and, in doing so, promising to avoid future negative feelings. If only it were that simple. Researchers investigating the difference between wanting what we have and having what we want found that satisfaction and pleasure from consumption are less about the object and more about the motivations associated with the experience of shopping. It's easy to succumb to temptation and buy something impulsively without considering the consequences. Psychologists working in fashion aim to educate and empower consumers to make more informed and considered purchasing decisions. This is in line with the British designer Dame Vivienne Westwood, who wisely encourages us, "Buy less. Choose well. Make it last. Quality, not quantity. Everybody's buying far too many clothes."[1]

SHOPPING FOR FASHION

Many modern societies are characterised by a strongly held belief that "to have is to be" such that individuals often define themselves and others in terms of their possessions. In the UK, shopping is one of the most popular leisure pursuits, although until the recent growth of interest in menswear, fashion shopping has tended to be a more popular pursuit for women than men. However, with the increased demand for male fashion and increased exposure to images of athletic male bodies, men are increasingly shopping for fashion as a leisure pastime. Nevertheless, women still shop for fashion more than men do. One reason for this is that from a very young age, females are judged on their appearance, and males on their skills and abilities. As a result, the goal of many girls and women is to look good, and so they are driven to seek clothing that shows them and their bodies in the best light. A positive aspect of fashion is that it can be used to alter appearance, express identity and boost confidence by enhancing positive aspects and concealing those we prefer to hide. Although we are seeing an increase in men's interest in consuming fashion, there is still some way to go until men and women find shopping for clothes and accessories equally pleasurable. In a 2013 paper, reported in the *Telegraph*, researchers reported that 80% of men said they hated shopping with their partner, and 45% said they avoided it at all costs.[2] The study's findings showed that half of all couples end up rowing when they go shopping together as men claim they get bored, hungry or thirsty and wish they were outside.

Clothing consumers may be shopping for utilitarian or hedonistic reasons. Those shopping for the former are likely to make a fast shopping trip. Those shopping for the latter derive pleasure from the shopping experience itself and therefore may savour it and make multiple purchases. Utilitarian clothing items offer protection from the climate and other aspects of the environment as well as optimising performance in extreme conditions, and this may not be simply a utilitarian purchase decision. The growing market in sportswear and outdoor gear which promises improved performance during extended exposure to the elements is testament to the increased demand for stylish and utilitarian items. This is driven in part by the fitspiration movement.

Over the past few years, along with the increased interest in health and wellbeing, an alternative to the thin ideal, the 'fit' body, is emerging for men and women. While this is intuitively likely to be physically healthier than aspiring to extreme thinness, any obsession with body or appearance can be considered psychologically unhealthy and can lead to mental health issues. 'Fitspiration', designed to inspire viewers towards a healthier lifestyle by promoting exercise and healthy food, is gaining momentum. An investigation of the impact of fitspiration images compared with travel images on women's body image found that despite seeming to be a positive innovation, fitspiration can also have negative unintended consequences for body image.[3] However, fashion has seized the opportunities presented as a result of the increased use of cycling as a means of urban transportation. Novel textiles and designs for protective clothing and helmets are emerging which can be considered fashionable. Associated with the fitspiration movement is the fashion concept of athleisure: athletic clothing worn for leisure. This has boosted the sportswear market to become one of the fastest growing of all fashion areas.

Fashion also enables us to protect our modesty by concealing specific parts of our bodies. Of course, what is considered modest or immodest is subjective and generally a function of the *zeitgeist*. Fashion has tended to oscillate between extremes of greater body exposure, particularly in female clothing, and modest fashion. Revealing clothing is designed with the aim of making women look sexier and, as a consequence, more attractive. However, this practice can reduce the concept of self-worth to a factor of how much skin is on show. Individual women will have a preference for how much they expose or hide certain parts of their bodies in certain contexts, and this preference is likely to be determined by socialisation and cultural influences. Increasingly, we are seeing more interest in what is termed *modest fashion*. Perhaps this is a backlash to the sexualisation of women and increasingly more men in fashion imagery or a desire to show explicitly our affiliations to religious or ethnic groups. We can also demonstrate affiliation via adornment and accessories. These may be in the form of physical alterations to the body such as piercings, tattoos or jewellery, or in the form of headwear, footwear, scarves, gloves, embellishments to clothing, bags and so on. Individuals may opt to use adornments to increase their attractiveness, status or feelings of self-worth. They also allow the wearer to adapt existing items of clothing to appear more distinct or fashionable. Furthermore, there are no sizing issues when buying accessories. Everyone can indulge their fashionable side regardless of any body issues. Every bag fits.

The essence of fashion is that it keeps reinventing itself. This appeals to consumers because the brain does not pay attention to the 'ordinary' or familiar; it focuses on the new and unfamiliar. Marketers use this knowledge to attract our attention. Novelty causes a number of brain systems to become activated, including the dopamine system. Dopamine is associated with the need for more rather than feeling good. Dopamine is implicated in many addictive behaviours such as addiction to chocolate, money, sex and possibly items of clothing. However, investigations with animals suggest that it is not the novelty *per se* that releases the dopamine, it is the motivation to seek novelty that increases dopamine levels. This is the fundamental principle of fashion and explains the insatiable nature of consumerism and the constant drive for new clothing.

The demand for both fast fashion and luxury brands is increasing despite the volatile economic climate. Consumers buy luxury items for many reasons including attaining or maintaining social status, demonstrating economic superiority, impressing others and provoking envy in others. High fashion is readily associated with branding. Recently, fashion models have become celebrities used to endorse products and brands. Fashion consumers may see models as 'super-consumers' who have successfully created identities to which they aspire. In turn, this affects consumers' perception of the product or brand especially when the characteristics of the product are congruent with the image portrayed by the celebrity. Celebrity endorsement is recognised as an effective method of communication, as celebrities have been found to be more powerful than anonymous actors. Celebrity endorsement is used to attract and gain attention to create favourable associations with the brand. Celebrity endorsement in advertising has been recognised as a ubiquitous feature of modern marketing.[4] In the UK and the USA, the use of celebrity endorsers is increasing as it has the potential to underpin global campaigns by creating a positive influence. Because celebrities who endorse a brand or product should be perceived as an expert in the category, models are perfect endorsers for fashion brands. Furthermore, because fashion models are typically attractive, they, like others who are perceived as attractive, are imbued with other positive and desirable characteristics and qualities. However, the impact on how strongly we are influenced to buy the product is mediated by how much we 'like' the celebrity endorsing it. In our celebrity culture, brands choose celebrities who portray the image and personality of the brand. This is the case in fashion as well as other industries, and in fashion it relates to clothing, perfumes and accessories. We're told by fashion magazines that we 'must have' the bags that celebrities are using, and because bags are not subject to 'fit', we can easily imagine ourselves using the same bag as a celebrity and therefore are easily influenced to want it, and ultimately buy it. Recently, bloggers and models with hundreds of thousands of followers on Instagram have taken over from celebrities in endorsing brands and products.

Conspicuous consumption is defined as spending money on and acquiring luxury goods and services to publicly display economic power and to compete with others.[5] More than a century ago, conspicuous consumption was criticised for being wasteful. Yet, today, anecdotal evidence suggests that at least 10% of clothing in women's wardrobes has never been worn or is no longer worn. The conspicuous consumption theory has been associated with trickle-down theories which state that fashion flows from the upper classes to the lower classes within society because people in lower social groups seek to attain higher status by imitating and adopting the fashions of those in higher social groups. As a result, those in higher social groups respond by adopting new fashions so that they remain differentiated.

In the 20th century, high fashion became more accessible across socio-economic strata. Recently, rather than trickling down from the top, high-status styles have developed from street style and youth subcultures. During the 1980s particularly, fashion labels previously associated with haute couture began producing ready-to-wear collections that were affordable to larger and more varied populations. These developments blurred the distinctions between markers of socio-economic status to some degree; however, materials can still differentiate between them. Interestingly, fashion has become so ubiquitous that it may now be termed *inconspicuous consumption*. The torn, worn-out jeans, T-shirts and so on which were prevalent among teens in the 1960s have become fashionable once again. The difference is that in the 1960s, jeans were worn until they were worn out, whereas today consumers buy brand new worn-out jeans.

Consumer psychologists have found that the most important factors when deciding what to buy are the product's extrinsic properties, such as price, brand name and store image, and intrinsic properties, such as style, colour, fabric, care, fit and quality, and that only a very small part of clothing preference is down to aesthetic evaluation.[6] However, clothing can take on symbolic meaning when it becomes attached to events. Women tend to form an attachment to clothes with symbolic meaning such as those that made them look and feel special, whereas men become attached to clothing that allows them to do something active, rather than based on how the clothes make them look or feel.

People who like to shop for fun are more likely to buy on impulse and then feel guilty about the purchase. Impulse buyers typically have difficulty controlling their emotions so it may be harder for them than others to resist the urge to buy. They may shop to avoid negative feelings such as emptiness, low self-esteem, insecurity, boredom, loneliness and anger; to pursue an unattainable ideal image; or to enhance others' perceptions of them. Indulging in shopping helps numb negative feelings, temporarily providing a feeling of control, but as distressing feelings recur, the urge to shop returns. However, psychologists have found that feeling guilty often drives us to pursue the vices we feel guilty about, rather than changing this behaviour as a result of feeling guilty. They claim this could be a result of feelings of sin and remorse, which can trigger thoughts of desire in the brain, which thus releases dopamine, driving us to seek more. Besides increasing attraction to temptation, the researchers claim that guilty feelings may also set off the feeling that a single lapse is licence to give up completely. If impulsive buying becomes a habit, it can become detrimental to the buyer's psychological, physical and social wellbeing and lead to compulsive buying disorder (CBD).

CBD typically starts in the late teens and early twenties, perhaps as a result of leaving home and acquiring a credit card for the first time. Estimates claim that up to 92% of people with CBD are women, although this gender difference may be a result of men being less likely to self-report.[7] In a random telephone survey of 2,513 adults conducted in the USA in 2006, researchers found that 5.8% of respondents self-categorised themselves as compulsive shoppers.[8] CBD is characterised by a preoccupation with shopping, feelings of tension or anxiety before the purchase, and a sense of relief following the purchase. However, despite the positive feelings initially associated with shopping, compulsive shoppers may also experience feelings of anxiety or guilt, which may result in returning items to the store and then shopping again. When this happens, and the shoppers can't find what they want, they are motivated to try even harder as levels of dopamine, the neurotransmitter associated with desire, continue to rise the longer the urge persists. This finding is supported by neuroscience, which suggests that CBD could be 'rewarded' by the release of endorphins and dopamine during the shopping experience, which over time becomes addictive.

Given the many social and cultural factors that increase the addictive potential of shopping and spending, it is not so surprising to learn that more than 15 million people in the USA are considered to have a shopping and spending addiction. Modern society's material focus combined with the availability of credit, and the accessibility of omnichannel shopping, encourages consumers to shop 24 hours a day. Compulsive shoppers are willing to pay whatever it takes to purchase whatever they want, and they go on shopping binges despite the negative consequences. They may hide or destroy price tags and receipts and lie about how much they have spent. This provides a sense of control, but in reality, the person is out of control as shopping addiction frequently leads to debt and sometimes bankruptcy. A lack of financial resources is not a deterrent as the desire for control, immediate gratification and freedom from stress, anxiety or depression is overpowering in addiction. In fact, a lack of money could exacerbate the addiction as a result of the stress it causes. The shopping and spending activity itself is associated with a feeling of happiness and power which is immediately, but temporarily, gratifying. After a few minutes, there may be after-effects of remorse and guilt. However, these drive the spender to purchase again and achieve that brief, but intense, emotional high.

Individuals with CBD may be constantly in search of the perfect or elusive item. Like impulsive shopping, CBD is associated with mood and anxiety disorders, substance abuse, eating disorders and other impulse control disorders. A study of 18 participants with CBD found that all but one had at least one first-degree relative with major depression; more than half had an alcohol or drug use problem; and three had an anxiety disorder.[9] Another study found that 137 first-degree relatives of 33 individuals with CBD were significantly more likely to have depression or any other psychological, alcohol or drug-related disorder than the general population.[10]

Although the use of selective serotonin reuptake inhibitors has been tried to stop CBD with this population, evidence suggests that the most effective treatment is attending therapy and support groups. CBD is not limited to people who spend beyond their means; it also includes people who spend an inordinate amount of time shopping or who think about buying things obsessively but never purchase them. However, compulsive shoppers often describe an increasing level of urgency or anxiety that can only be resolved by making a purchase. The pace of the fashion industry means that novelty is never far away. This especially true of the fast fashion market.

SUSTAINABLE FASHION

Sustainable fashion is a counter movement to fast fashion which developed in the USA from a product-driven concept in the 1980s to a market-based process in the late 1990s. Problems in the fashion industry have become glaringly apparent as a result of moving fashion manufacturing and production from local sites to the Far East. Chemicals used in dyes pollute rivers when they are washed out, and cotton production demands precious land and water resources that could be used in a more socially responsible way. Add to these the poor working conditions reported in sweatshop scandals, and it is not difficult to sympathise with the sustainable fashion philosophy of reducing the environmental impact of fashion. One problem for the sustainability agenda is the fast fashion industry.

Fast fashion contributes to overconsumption and is based on the brand's desire for profit and consumers' desire for new clothing. With more and more collections being designed each year, fashion soon becomes obsolescent. To meet consumer demands to wear the latest fashion, fast fashion brands provide affordable, fashionable designs which are copied from the catwalk and made available within hours online and instore. In order to achieve this, the supply chain needs to be fast and cheap. The aim is to allow ordinary fashion consumers to buy the latest fashion styles at a lower price. Fast fashion has become associated with cheap, disposable fashion and a source of environmental damage. The slow fashion movement, which developed in opposition to fast fashion, alleges that the manufacturing and production processes used by fast fashion contribute to social and environmental damage. Because of the cheap price and availability, the quality is often poor. Yet consumers are tempted to buy more than they need because of the cheap price, leading to overconsumption. But because of its low quality, fast fashion items often need to be replaced more often than higher quality counterparts. This also contributes to overconsumption. Consequently, unsold stock, and clothing that has been worn once or a few times, is disposed of, often ending up in landfill sites.

The average UK household spends about £1,700 a year on clothes but wears only 70% of them. An estimated £140 million worth of clothes are sent to the landfill every year, the majority from fast fashion brands. Sustainable fashion activists argue that every manufactured item or service we buy is detrimental to the environment. Their rhetoric emphasises how individuals need to question not only whether they can afford a particular purchase or experience, but also whether the planet can afford to provide it. They assert that consumers need to realise that psychological wellbeing does not result from material wealth. Research has found that one's standard of living has much less bearing on happiness than the attitudes, values and expectations we bring to the way we live. Awareness-raising about the detrimental consequences of fast fashion has been on the agenda for more than a decade, yet change is very slow. Fast fashion brands continue to be the biggest earners, and poor working conditions are perpetuated while the environment continues to suffer.

Estimates claim that more than 1 million tonnes of textiles are thrown away every year in the UK alone. At least 50% of these are recyclable, but only 25% are recovered for recycling processes. Recovering more textile and clothing waste would reduce demand for landfill sites as well as natural resources. Some fashion brands including Patagonia, Marks and Spencer, and Armani jeans are using recycled materials in their fashion production systems, and individual consumers can make fashion more sustainable by upcycling and recycling their clothes. Upcycling is the cost-effective, creative process of creating something new and improved from some thing or things that exist already. By definition, upcycling is sustainable as it reduces clothing and textile waste to create new items. It is also cost-effective. Recycling involves extending the life of existing clothing through taking it to charity shops, selling it through car boot sales or online trading sites, contributing it to clothing swap shops and bringing it to store take-back campaigns. An article published in *Nature* in 2016 argues that frugal innovation must become ubiquitous and rewarded if we are to redress the imbalance between overproduction and demand.[11] Consumers and producers can achieve this through conspicuous non-consumption as the new signifier of self-worth.

The continued popularity of vintage fashion means that recycled clothing is given a new lease of life with a new owner. However, while some people see vintage clothing as a treasured find, for example clothes which bring nostalgia for past times, others may see vintage clothing as old, disposed-of garments whose owners no long want them or have passed away. When we love vintage, we find the searching and finding experience as pleasurable as wearing the garment. When we don't, we apply negative associations and do not even want to touch the garments. There may be many different reasons for these differences, but one potential candidate is the idea of contagion. Just as we are influenced by celebrity endorsement and brand personality (positive contagion), we can be influenced by negative contagion such as that associated with a garment's previous owner or association. Contagion in this sense is related to the psychological concept of essentialism. Psychological essentialism underpins the basic building blocks of cognition: categorisation. It is the belief that an intangible, internal and unseen essence determines the shared outward appearances and behaviours of category members. This concept has been investigated with regard to acceptance of replacement children's toys[12] and organ transplants,[13] in which the findings showed that individuals believed that an organ transplant would result in a change of personality for the receiver to that of the donor. When asked about recipients of a donated pig's heart, as is now used in organ transplantation, participants reported that the receiver would become more pig-like but would not become a pig. Applying this concept to second-hand clothing, it is logical to assume that some individuals may believe they will take on the essence of the item if they wear it.

The anti-fast fashion movement is often cited as saying buy less and spend more on better quality items. But expensive clothes do not necessarily come with a guarantee of ethics. As mentioned, producers of cheap fashion are generally seen as perpetuating low wages and poor working conditions so their clothing can be sold at very cheap prices.

Ethically and socially responsible consumers are likely to spend more on clothing items in the understanding that expensive clothes are an ethical option. However, the 2015 Clean Clothes Campaign report claims that workers in many countries are paid far below minimum wage not only by fast fashion producers but also by some luxury brands including Versace, Dolce and Gabbana, Armani and Max Mara. Conditions in many European counties are unacceptable.[14] The Clean Clothes Campaign works with garment workers all over the world. While many people are aware of the terrible working conditions and poverty wages for garment workers in Asia, the 2014 report *Stitched Up* debunks the myth that "Made in Europe" means better conditions for workers. In a 2016 report, *Labour on a Shoe String*, the Clean Clothes Campaign team report the endemic and systemic problems associated with shoe and clothing production across six European countries.[15] The reports make for sorry, but necessary reading.

Another unpleasant development that is not restricted to fast fashion is the demand for 'see now, buy now' fashion. High-end brands have responded to competition from online companies such as Amazon who deliver within hours. The assumption is that consumers, and their target market in particular, do not wait. A recent article in the *New York Times'* "Fashion and Style" section laments how technology has enabled designer goods to be delivered to consumers in 90 minutes in 10 major cities around the world.[16] Fashion companies Farfetch, Net-a-Porter and Matchesfashion.com offer a global same-day service and even a 90-minute service in London. These retailers argue that they need to meet the demands of Generation X and Y, who, according to them, are not prepared to wait for their items. According to Farfetch, their consumers rank timely delivery as the most important option. This is not surprising since Farfetch offers fast delivery and its customers are likely to value this service above other factors.

This section has discussed one of the darker sides of fashion production and fashion consumption. But it is possible to make our clothes work for us, to enable our clothing to enhance our wellbeing. Two studies which investigated this possibility are described below.

CLOTHING FOR WELLBEING

Poor employment conditions, overconsumption and the very narrow stereotype of beauty promoted by the industry have ethical implications that have remained unchallenged. Psychologists can collaborate with professionals working in the fashion industry to promote a more inclusive and diverse representation of what is 'beautiful' through applying psychological science to understand these important problems and predict and ultimately change behaviour. Direct influences include exposure to fashion imagery. Therefore, understanding how to build and maintain resilience against such influences has never been more necessary. The final part of this chapter discusses some of the few research papers that have applied positive psychology to enhance wellbeing through clothing.

Despite the problems in the industry, fashion has been and continues to be a vehicle for positive change. Many projects by fashion professionals have successfully raised awareness globally of many important issues in fashion, from sustainability to climate change. However, an analysis of the evidence for these projects' and campaigns' impact on behaviour is often overlooked. Recently, however, psychologists have taken this on board and are now working on understanding human behaviour and ways to lead people to make the necessary changes to improve, or even eradicate, such issues through fashion. The next section looks at the emerging literature on how clothing can be used to enhance wellbeing and encourage sustainable practices in fashion consumers.

The area of attachment to clothing has received great interest within the fashion industry with many websites, books and artworks exploring the notion of clothing attachment. In addition, experts within sustainable design have discussed how relationships with clothing can be developed through the application of the framework of emotionally durable design. Others have discussed how the connection between wearer and garment can increase the longevity of ownership. In psychology, attachment between adults and their special possessions has been studied, and although attachment is seen as multifaceted and complex, many existing studies suggest a one-dimensional construct which can change over time. However, little is known about attachment to clothing from a psychological perspective. To address this gap in knowledge, Fleetwood-Smith previously demonstrated the potential for enhancing wellbeing by encouraging individuals to create personal symbolic meaning for particular items of clothing.[17] Fleetwood-Smith, Mair and Hefferon extended this work, suggesting that building relationships with our clothing and understanding an item's essence can enable us to value and savour it.[18] The rationale for this research is based on the closely related cognitive psychological concepts of enclothed cognition and essentialism. Essentialism describes the belief that particular objects have a set of defining, yet intangible, characteristics which make them what they are. Enclothed cognition is defined as the systematic influence that beliefs about clothing have on the wearer's psychological processes dependent on the co-occurrence of the symbolic meaning and the physical experience of wearing the clothes.[19] Taken together, these psychological processes have a powerful influence on cognition with as yet undefined potential to benefit wellbeing and improve sustainability in fashion. Fleetwood-Smith et al. found that when a garment had symbolic significance personal to its wearer, they wanted to preserve the garment and would not replace the garment even with an exact replica.[20] Their participants claimed that the garment had developed human-like qualities which enabled it to act as an extension of the self, thus enhancing psychological wellbeing.

Zoe Shaughnessy studied the lived experience of women living with breast cancer as they navigated the landscape of living with an altered body, and their relationship with their identity and dress, which emerged through everyday practices of selecting, trying on and wearing clothing.[21] Shaughnessy conducted semi-structured interviews with six female breast cancer survivors aged 39 to 59 years who had undergone a mastectomy, and also screened them for post-traumatic growth. The findings, analysed using interpretative phenomenological analysis, highlighted the women's relationship with clothing as manifested through four emergent themes. Firstly, clothing could be used as a means to manage mood, a way to feel better about themselves. Secondly, clothing could be a positive and uplifting source of connecting with others that enabled the women to make new friendships and rebuild former relations through uniting around clothing struggles and triumphs. Thirdly, clothing was used as a means to conceal, reveal, accentuate and compensate through its flexibility. In doing so, it eased the impact of the breast cancer journey. Finally, the women used clothing as a way of exploring the self: they "played with" clothing and "tried on" a "new" self. Shaughnessy argues that in navigating the physical, psychological and social aspects of an altered self, the relationship the women formed with clothing was complex. She concludes that for the participants clothing emerged as an active way of coping and a potential facilitator for creating an environment, and a means by which, to increase posttraumatic growth. These findings support previous research which shows that women with better body image perceptions have higher levels of self-confidence in coping with breast cancer. In doing so, Shaughnessy's work lays the foundation for further studies examining the therapeutic potential of clothing within the management of long-term conditions and in day-to-day wellbeing. Furthermore, by shining a light on the lived experience of women living with breast cancer, this work demonstrates how fashion designers contribute to enhanced wellbeing among those living with breast cancer, thus raising the potential of fashion way above its connotations of superficiality and frivolity.

SUMMARY

This chapter has considered the psychology of shopping for fashion, the concept of sustainable fashion and clothing for wellbeing. It explored the notion of contagion and psychological essentialism in relation to sustainable fashion, discussing why recycling and reusing may not appeal to everyone. Following this, the concept of shopping for fashion as a leisure pursuit was introduced. This led to a discussion about how this can lead to unhealthy shopping behaviour that could even be described as an addiction. When this happens, compulsive shopping behaviour can be described as a mental health problem. As we've seen, clothing and fashion serve multiple purposes, one of which is the role they can play in enhancing wellbeing.

6

FASHION AND BEHAVIOUR

OVERVIEW

We dress for many reasons: to protect and adorn the body, to extend its abilities and to communicate psychological and physical aspects of our self and identity via nonverbal, visual communication. There are many individual, societal and cultural differences in fashion, in clothing in general and particularly in the meanings that our clothing elicits. As we are motivated to belong to social groups, we use what we wear to communicate our affiliations. We can also use our clothing to empower us and even to enhance our thinking.

WHY WE WEAR WHAT WE WEAR

As discussed previously in this book, what we choose to wear is determined by many factors including our personality, mood and emotions as well as the context. Formal clothing is often worn to adhere to social norms, for example, where it is considered important to feel respected and perceived as professional. Although there is a dearth of literature from psychology attempting to explain the psychology of what we wear, it is not a new endeavour. Early social scientists were concerned with the social stratification in their modern society that drove fashion. They argued that clothing cannot and does not mean the same thing to all people at all times, and therefore what is worn represents symbolic class and status boundaries.

Simmel argued that individuals have a psychological tendency towards imitation because it needs "no personal and creative appreciation".[1] Imitation also affords effortless belonging. According to Simmel, fashion satisfies that demand for social adaptation in which an individual can be simply an example. It also satisfies the need for differentiation, particularly with regard to social strata. Simmel argued that the clothing worn by the different social strata is never the same because the upper classes abandon the fashion as soon as it is adopted by the lower classes. However, recently, street fashion has led the way with wealthy people adopting the style of the lower classes. In Simmel's critique of fashion as "ugly and repugnant things are that sometimes in vogue", he argues that the desire of fashion is to get its consumers to adopt the "the most atrocious things for its sake alone". He reasons that the reason "aesthetically impossible styles seem distingue, elegant and artistically tolerable" is that the person wearing them has paid a great deal of attention to their appearance and is in fact elegant.[2]

Clothing and other appearance-objects, including hairstyles, make-up, accessories and facial and bodily characteristics, allow us to interpret abstract social processes such as understanding how people relate to each other. Although socialisation, culture and gender may lead people to think differently about clothes, we all wear clothes, and whether we like it or not, what we wear is an expression of who we are. The way our clothing 'sits' on our bodies, the way we move and talk, our habitus can help others determine who we are.[3]

These facets of our identity are socialised by family and the social groups to which we belong. In addition, our skin, hair and teeth are increasingly symbols of class while all aspects of appearance, including style, contribute to aesthetic appreciation.

Style includes physical elements of the item of clothing (textile, cut, colour and so on) as well as the combination and arrangement of items of clothing and may be considered a factor of personal expression and social norms influenced by an individual's dominant values. Particular historical 'movements' have been represented by particular styles. For example, modernism, which was dominant in the early and middle years of 20th century, represented a movement away from previous styles towards novelty. Modernism is related to scientific and technological advances and may be considered a result of the cognitive psychology revolution and the advances in technology that ensued as a result of World War II. These days there are few occasions when only one particular item of clothing can be considered appropriate, but limits are imposed by the situation, culture and society even though we may choose to ignore them.

In 1929, Hurlock investigated the notion of motivation in fashion. She asked more than 1400 people aged between 16 and 51 if they dressed (i) to please their own sex or the opposite sex, (ii) to appear prosperous, or (iii) to enhance their physical assets, and whether modesty was a factor in clothing choice.[4] In contrast to the claims made by Veblen, 20 years earlier, concerning conspicuous consumption, Hurlock found that people did not dress to look prosperous, but to please their own sex, to be modest and to enhance their physical features. A 1934 survey with 350 women investigated their fashion desires in relation to conformity, economy, comfort, modesty, self-expression, sex and femininity and found that looking prosperous was not an objective.[5] Rather, desire to conform was strongest, followed by maximising personal appearance and then self-expression. Conformity is closely related to the need for social identity as both concepts involve the internalisation of group beliefs and attitudes. Of course, times change, and if these studies were to be replicated today, the findings might be very different. Nevertheless, the desire to conform can lead us to change our behaviour and beliefs in response to perceived group pressure, as demonstrated in three classic psychology studies. These studies examining conformity of judgements and opinions in groups demonstrate how people conform because it is easier to do so than to face the consequences of going against the majority.[6] Conformity can also manifest with regard to clothing, resulting in the benefits of better group acceptance and cohesiveness. However, other studies have found more positive reactions to people who broke established norms slightly.[7] For example, a man wearing a red bow-tie to a black-tie event was viewed as having higher status and competence than others. Valuing uniqueness also increased ratings of the status and competence of a professor who wore red Converse sneakers while giving a lecture. A meta-analysis of 109 studies found that dress communicated characteristics including competence, power, intelligence, sociability and mood.[8] Furthermore, dress has been found to influence perception of intelligence and academic potential for both students and teachers.[9]

Both men and women rate women wearing a provocative dress as more sexually appealing and more attractive, but less faithful in marriage, more likely to engage in sexual teasing, more likely to use sex for personal gain, more likely to be sexually experienced and, worryingly, more likely to be raped than when wearing conservative dress.[10] Others have found that women who dress provocatively are considered responsible for sexual assaults and experiences of sexual harassment that happened to them.[11]

When we try on new clothing, we can see ourselves as a different person and take on a new identity and mood. Studies investigating the relationships between perception of mood, self-consciousness and the selection of clothing among male and female students have found that females are more sensitive to different mood states and self-consciousness in comparison to males, which affects their choice of clothing. The colour of clothing also affected the mood of the wearer and the observer. Many other factors that elicit an emotional as well as a cognitive response impinge on clothing preference. These include physical features such as skin response, size and shape of the item, thermal comfort, fit, how much of the body the item reveals or conceals and other visual features; the wearer's self-appearance; and associative reasons and memories.

A recent study explored relationships between clothing style, preference, personality factors, emotions and mood to understand the psychological profile of the fashion consumer when trying on casual, formal or eveningwear outfits with differences in fit, colour, revealing aspects, brand and fabric types.[12] Hair was tied back so as not to influence perceptions, and shoes were flat or heeled, 'worn as appropriate'. The researchers surveyed 27 female students with regard to emotion, mood and personality before and after they tried on the eight outfits. The participants then ranked the eight outfits in order of preference. Results showed that mood was a more important factor in preferences than personality and that feeling well-dressed led to feelings of greater sociability, power and worth. In addition, wearing casual outfits made participants feel more active than the other outfits.

An interest in the relationship between clothing and mood was heightened with the release of the Hollywood blockbuster *La La Land*. At the time (winter 2017), the fashion industry was promoting bright colours on the catwalk (such as orange at Armani, scarlet at Maison Margiela and yellow and pink at Giambattista Valli) as well as in cosmetics. In the wake of the film's success the stores filled with yellow clothing; consumers were told that wearing yellow would make them happy. In an interview for an article in the UK's national press, entitled "Dopamine Dressing", which led with the notion that wearing yellow could lift the wearer's mood, I explained that the symbolic meaning of the clothing could potentially lift mood, but the wearer has to believe in this.[13] Therefore, the mood-enhancing power lies with the wearer, not the clothing or its colour *per se*. Because the meaning of colour is culturally and socially constructed, interpreting its 'meaning' is subjective and dependent on multiple factors, as discussed further in the next section. Because we behave partially in response to others' feedback, wearing an item which engenders positive responses will make us feel good. Ultimately, colour matters as far as the symbolic meaning we attribute to it and the degree to which we believe in its powers.

Colour perception results from subjective interpretation of the wavelength of light reflected from objects combined with cultural associations and our assumptions and experiences. We live in an atmosphere of electro-magnetic waves including microwaves, x-rays and light. Light waves are the only part of the spectrum that humans can see. When light strikes an object, it is reflected back to the retina.

The wavelengths that get absorbed by the object or that are reflected from it depend on the features of the object, such as texture and colour, and the nature of the light source illuminating it. The reflected light waves are processed by our visual system. Processing and interpreting visual information involves many complex processes. However, because we see in a way that is seemingly automatic, we often take vision for granted, and many people are surprised to know that vision is in fact a psychological as well as physical process. Vision is psychological because we need to interpret the sensory information that comes from the environment. In the case of vision, these are light waves. However, its automaticity belies its complexity. How we make sense of objects as coherent wholes, separate from other objects, remains an intriguing area of research in psychology as well as neuroscience and philosophy.

From a physical perspective, light waves enter the eye via the cornea and then the lens. The lens focuses light onto the retina at the back of the eye, where it is converted into electrical impulses. The retina comprises photoreceptive cells known as rods and cones, which detect the photons of light and respond with neural impulses. The neural impulses are then processed via complex feed-forward and feedback processes in multiple brain areas. However, the perception of objects, and indeed of their colour, depends on perception, the meaning we bring to the sensory information we process. Visual information is processed in multiple brain areas and the exact process by which this happens is still not fully understood. A simple interpretation would be to assume that perception takes place in a linear fashion through the brain's structures to the visual cortex, which is situated at the back of the brain, but the process does not stop there. In order to make sense of this information, we use our motivations, experiences and expectations. This explains how different individuals perceive the same object, or even features of the same object, as different. One feature that can be and is perceived differently by individuals is colour, and an excellent example of the complexity of interpreting colour in relation to fashion is 'the dress'.

In 2015, a photo of a dress was posted on a social networking site, Tumblr. It caused a stir because of the different perceptions it triggered in different viewers. Some people saw the dress as white and gold and others as blue and black. The discussions around these reactions varied and triggered research studies by psychologists and neuroscientists. An influential study reported in the journal *Cortex* found that the different perceptions depended on many factors.[14] Using functional magnetic resonance imaging, the researchers asked 28 participants to look at the image of the dress and images of large coloured squares that matched two of the colours in the dress while their brains were being scanned.

Remember that the light waves that are reflected back to the eye comprise reflected light from the object and the light source illuminating it. In order to interpret the colour, we need to disentangle these two sources. Typically, we do this well through a process known as colour constancy, which describes how we perceive objects as the same colour even under different lighting conditions. Imagine you see your red dressing gown in your darkened bedroom; it now looks grey, but you know it's red because you bring your knowledge and experience to bear on the sensory information presented to you. Cognitive psychologists describe this process as "discounting the illuminant". That is, we ignore the information coming from the light source and rely on our experience to decipher the colour of the object.

As the case of 'the dress' illustrates very well, perception of colour is subjective and therefore can vary from person to person. The researchers found variations in brain activation between those who perceived the dress as blue and black and those who perceived it as white and gold, and variations in brain activation between viewing the images of the coloured squares and viewing the dress (the former without context, the latter with context). The participants who perceived the dress as white and gold showed heightened activation in many different brain areas, but this was not found when they viewed the images of the coloured squares. The researchers argued that the heightened activity was a result of the participants' interpretative processing when looking at the dress that they did not engage in when looking at the coloured squares. That is, the viewers who saw the dress as white and gold engaged their assumptions and expectations, as well as the raw sensory information from the environment, to interpret colour. However, what distinguishes this illusion from other visual illusions is that it is impossible to switch from one understanding to the other. In the duck-rabbit illusion, viewers perceive either the duck or the rabbit, but it is possible to switch perception so that each is visible independently. The researchers argue that the inability to switch views may be the underlying reason it is so difficult to change some people's minds.

Metaphors such as *seeing red, seeing the light* and *feeling blue* are common in language. While it may not be too problematic to understand the metaphorical meaning of these words, it is difficult to translate the metaphorical meaning of clothing through its colour as there are so many mediating factors. However, studies based on evolutionary theory and social learning theory lend some support to understanding the influences of colour on psychological functioning. As Elliot argues, most work on the colour of clothing has focused on red.[15] He argues that other colours and a range of associated factors such as colour properties, viewers' distance and angle, amount and type of ambient light, and the presence of other colours have been largely ignored. For these reasons, reports that a certain colour of clothing represents a certain characteristic aligned with a verbal language equivalent should be considered with caution.

Colour has been a source of fascination in many disciplines since Goethe's (1810) *Theory of Colours*, in which colour categories were associated with emotional responses (e.g., red with warmth or excitement).[16] Researchers have found that particular colours produce specific physiological reactions that result in emotional experience, cognitive orientation and overt action. Specifically, colours with longer wavelengths feel arousing or warm, whereas shorter wavelength colours feel relaxing or cool. Red is particularly interesting in terms of arousal as visual sensitivity to skin redness that has been induced in a lab setting has been interpreted as a signal of aggression, anger, embarrassment or sexual arousal. People have evolutionary and culturally created associations between colours and affect, cognition and behaviour. For example, viewing a woman wearing red or having red near her enhanced heterosexual males' attraction to that woman.[17]

The colours red and black have been equally associated with higher attractiveness judgements when images of males were judged by men or women, and when men judged images of women, but not when women judged images of other women. Interestingly, significant correlations between clothing colour and attractiveness associations were found even when the colour of the clothing was obscured from those making the judgements, and when it was held constant by digital manipulation. To explain this, the researchers reasoned that clothing colour has a psychological influence on wearers as much as it does on the observers. They continued that the psychological influence on wearers influences attractiveness judgements by others rather than the actual colour of the clothing.[18] This explanation demonstrates that if we believe in the symbolic meaning of the clothing, for example that wearing red makes us more attractive, we can actually feel more attractive and therefore be perceived as more attractive by observers. This finding has been supported by researchers, who found that red-coloured clothing influenced subconscious perceptions of dominance in a simulated sports context for both the person wearing red and the observer regardless of whether they were men or women.[19] These researchers considered the influence of red on perception and behaviour to be so strong that they questioned whether red clothing should be regulated in sport. Furthermore, simply viewing red on oneself or others has been found to increase appraisals of aggressiveness and dominance. In aggressive encounters, humans experience a testosterone surge which produces visible facial reddening. Projecting this to non-human objects, researchers found that wearing red in an aggressive situation such as a sport contest conveys dominance and leads to a competitive advantage. For example, wrestlers wearing red are more likely to win their match.[20] However, the red advantage could be a factor of the referee's perceptual bias towards the colour red, according to other researchers.[21]

Black is one of fashionistas' most favoured colours for clothing, yet there is little empirical evidence about the reasons we wear black other than the finding that wearing red or black results in a person being judged as more attractive. This means that other people often make assumptions about us based on the colour of our clothes. Despite the cultural associations of colour, in the world of sport, black clothing is perceived as aggressive; in the world of fashion, black is chic. The little black dress is a fashion staple. It is suitable for any occasion, always smart, sexy and yet demure. It can be short or calf length, with straps, bandeau or sleeves. Regardless of silhouette, the little black dress is always stylish with timeless appeal that can reveal and hide simultaneously, suggesting elegance, class and style. It says the wearer knows how to dress for the occasion. Psychologically we might assume that someone wearing a little black dress prefers to be noticed for herself rather than her clothing; however, this would depend on the cut and silhouette of the dress. Because it's so versatile, it's possible to have plunging or high necklines, short or longer hemlines and strapless or sleeved styles. The meaning of the dress will depend on the silhouette, and that in turn is determined by what the wearer wants to expose and what she wants to conceal. Originally designed by Chanel and Patou, the little black dress was intended to be accessible to a wide range of consumers. Chanel started the little black dress trend with a long-sleeved woollen black dress designed for day wear, and an evening version in crepe, satin or velvet. Many variations have appeared since. Chanel grew up in an orphanage after losing her parents and claimed that the little black dress allowed the character of the wearer to show. The little black dress can be dressed up with jewellery such that the jewellery is more evident than the dress. This isn't possible with fussy or patterned clothing. Black was and still is associated with mourning, and around the time of the original creation of the little black dress, many women were wearing black in mourning for their loved ones killed during World War I. Research suggests that the little black dress was preferred in Hollywood even after colour film became available because colours tended to become distorted on film.

The leading characters in *Sex and the City* often wore little black dresses. Each character had a strong personality: Carrie was romantic and often wore designer outfits which matched her flirty, fun and romantic personality. However, Sarah Jessica Parker recently launched her own range which includes a little black dress with sleeves and a calf-length circular skirt, and another with a net tutu skirt. Samantha Jones was the 'man eater' in *Sex and the City*. She was often dressed in tight, bodycon styles that showed off her figure. Although Miranda, a reluctant mother, was typically dressed in a gender fluid way, she was also seen in a little black dress with a plunging neckline. This suggested her confidence and willingness to take risks when looking for fun. Finally, Charlotte, who was always keen to marry and have children, could be appropriately dressed in a demure little black dress with classy jewellery and shoes. The range of variations of the little black dress means every woman can own at least one. We can see this variety in many contexts, for example Madame X, the eponymous subject of a painting by John Singer Sergeant who was known for her beauty and was painted at Sergeant's request. Later the portrait was reworked to make the strap sit on her shoulder rather than have it slipped off. The shoulder strap off the shoulder looks sexier than on the shoulder. The viewer is left to imagine whether or not Madame X wanted to be portrayed that way.

As shown, colour is an important feature of fashion. Armani, Maison Margiela and Giambattista Valli showed bright colours in their autumn/winter 2017 collections, accentuated by cosmetics in bright rainbow colours. The notion behind these bright fashions was that they could lift the consumer's mood in the dark days of the UK winter. There is some validity to this notion, but only if the wearer believes in the symbolic meaning of the colour. This notion is explained later in this chapter, but for now we turn to clothing in the workplace and find that the advice to "dress for the job you want, not the job you have" actually has some scientific grounding.

Employees typically often make a significant effort to find out and adhere to dress codes at work in order to gain social acceptance and status and avoid disapproval, ridicule and exclusion. A study found that wearing a formal business suit as opposed to casual clothing enhances abstract cognitive processing and changes how objects, people and events are construed.[22] Indeed, people who wear formal clothes describe themselves as more competent and rational. Furthermore, what you wear can influence the outcomes of negotiations. When male participants were asked to wear either jogging bottoms or a business suit, before negotiating with a partner wearing their own clothing and unaware of the clothing manipulation, wearing the business suit led to higher testosterone levels and more profitable deals than wearing the jogging bottoms.[23]

Social class plays a pivotal role in the transition from school to work. It impacts the way in which working-class young adults make meaning of their vocational lives. Although participants from high and low socio-economic groups wanted more from their work lives, those from the higher group were motivated by intrinsic factors (satisfaction etc.) and those from the lower group extrinsically, for economic survival. Socio-economic status may also influence how much effort is spent preparing for an interview (including appearance management), but ultimately, if you can't afford the clothes that will give the appropriate impression, you are disadvantaged. Most disadvantaged women lack the financial resources necessary to enhance their outward appearance as an impression management technique, which therefore reduces their ability to obtain a good job. Disadvantaged women may need assistance with clothing for job interviews and for the workplace; the charity Dress for Success[24] helps women on welfare to obtain work-appropriate clothing at discount prices to facilitate their obtaining and retaining work.

Men have traditionally held positions of power in the workplace and therefore are more accepted in those roles with less questioning of their ability. Men are judged less on their appearance, more on their effectiveness, and, as discussed, women tend to be more concerned about their appearance than men are. Women have faced sex-based discrimination at work and outside although, thankfully, this is beginning to change, albeit slowly. As noted, the multiple features of what we wear interact and affect perceptions, expectations and responses to job applicants and roles in the workplace. We categorise and stereotype to be efficient in terms of cognitive processing, but this can also lead to serious errors in judgement. We form opinions about people very quickly and make judgements about their characters, personalities, intelligence and scholastic achievement in under a second based solely on appearance. For example, implicit personality theory, in which we assume that "what is beautiful is good", suggests that once a person is classified as attractive or unattractive, the observer links several personality characteristics associated with that social category to the individual. This is also known as the halo effect, which is discussed later in this chapter.

There exists a greater choice for women than men in terms of what is considered appropriate business clothing, which can be a blessing or a curse. Findings from studies with college students found that women were more concerned about their work clothes and associated a classic business suit with convention and dominance more than men did. Before a woman becomes established in her career and when she has freedom to choose what to wear to work, wearing a business suit may be considered as compensating for an incomplete professional self-image. However, as women become more established professionally, they are more likely to experiment with their work clothing and adopt ideas from fashion magazines and other media.

The clothing worn by a job applicant is perceived as a sign of status, power and ability and may determine success in the interview and on the job. Research has found that physical attractiveness, personal appearance and image influence organisations' employment decisions regarding hiring and promotion. Shockingly, some organisations have discriminated intentionally and explicitly on the basis of image (e.g., Abercrombie and Fitch), while others may be unaware of the influence and impact of image norms on their recruitment and selection policies. Image norms may be held implicitly in companies with easily identified organisational images (individuals' reaction to or knowledge, beliefs and feelings about a company). Recent findings suggest image issues may be more common for workers in the retail, entertainment and hospitality industries, where their jobs involve extensive contact with customers and the public. Companies in these types of industries may attempt to hire employees whose image is consistent with their organisational image. In such organisations, physically attractive employees receive more positive evaluations than unattractive counterparts in multiple areas including hiring, promotion and salary. However, research has found that, above all, the dress of the applicant exerts a consistent influence. In comparison with the dress of the applicant, physical attractiveness, the type of job applied for and the sex of the hiring agent had only a slight effect on ratings. Perhaps this is why job interviews are such a poor predictor of employee success in the role.

Leading figures in fashion and other industries are opting to wear a sort of uniform to work. People at the top are short on time. They do not wish to spend time and valuable cognitive resources on what they are going to wear. Rather, they choose to use them efficiently on what they consider to be more pressing issues. In reality, it is unlikely that our work colleagues would notice if we wore the same clothes every day. Our visual system is programmed to notice objects that are different, rather than those that are the same. From an evolutionary perspective, our attention is drawn to difference as a signal of a potential danger. Mark Zuckerberg's desire for simplicity in his clothing choice enables him to free up cognitive space for the more important and urgent matters he needs to deal with. Fashion thought leaders also like to wear work uniforms. Consider *Vogue* USA's editor Anna Wintour's shift dresses and New York creative director Matilda Kahl's white shirt and black trouser uniform. Those who have made it to the top, as opposed to those who are striving to reach the top, are likely to care more about performance than being perceived as looking attractive. The most important task is doing a great job.

FASHION AS COMMUNICATION

The emphasis on fashion as communication has received support through analogy with linguistics, so much so that parallels from clothing to the basic elements of a linguist grammar – code, syntax and semantics – have been drawn,[25] However, McCracken and Roth argue that interpretation is concerned with the whole appearance, not clothing in isolation. They argue that the interpretation of appearance is dependent on the specific context, if anyone cares enough to interpret it.[26] Therefore, what is considered the height of fashion is perceived as such only if those perceiving it are aware of fashion. Indeed, Boultwood and Jerrard's explanation of historic psychoanalytic accounts of fashion describes how body and clothing communication is a mix of contradictory multi-messages which create ambiguity for the observer and the wearer.[27] Consequently, it is difficult for individuals to predict how their clothing will be perceived as they are unable to check for common understanding or explain what was actually intended.

Communication involves the transmission of a message between a sender and a receiver. However, the process of communication is complex. Although Shannon's information theory has been criticised for ignoring the context in which communication takes place, and the reciprocal nature of communication, it serves well in the context of face-to-face communication and when considering the communicative nature of appearance.[28] Put simply, Shannon's information theory explains how 'noise' within the transmission process interferes with the message such that what is received may be different to what was sent. Noise in information theory refers to redundant or ambiguous elements that can be introduced at any stage in the communication process as a result of multiple factors. These are the intended message itself, the sender, the medium of sending and the receiver. Research has found that interpretation is a complex mixture of multiple cognitive and behavioural factors including attention, empathy, fashion knowledge, experience, expectations and the full range of the perceiver's individual differences. It is therefore unsurprising that communication by means of clothing is ambiguous at best and incomprehensible at worst.

The inaccuracy associated with interpreting visual and other non-verbal communication is well-documented and is relevant when considering the accuracy of judging others by their appearance. Errors arise in part as a result of the heuristics we use when making the judgements. Heuristics are an example of cognitive bias in which an impression created in one area tends to influence opinion in another area (e.g., as in stereotyping). We use heuristics in order to manage the deluge of sensory information from the environment that we face constantly. If we were to analyse every sensation, rather than using heuristics, we would exhaust our limited cognitive capacity. Also, we tend to be lazy thinkers, and thinking analytically demands the limited resource of attention. We tend to save this for novel or threatening situations. In most situations, using heuristics is not a problem. Even if the outcome is not perfect, it typically suffices. That is, it will do. However, when accuracy matters more than time, heuristics can lead us to make poor decisions that can have detrimental outcomes. We make judgements about others based on their appearance in a matter of milliseconds. Then, in addition to deciding whether or not they are attractive and whether or not we like them, we imbue them with many psychological characteristics based solely on their appearance. This is known as the halo effect, in which an outcome in one area is due to factors derived from another. The halo effect is another example of a cognitive bias. But our clothes do more than send and reflect an impression of who we are. Recent findings show that our clothes can do more than influence how others judge us; they can influence how we feel and how we think. This exciting development of the concept of embodied cognition is known as enclothed cognition. Both embodied and enclothed cognition are discussed in the final subsection of this chapter.

Umberto Eco claimed he 'spoke through his clothes', suggesting that clothing communicates through a process akin to spoken or written language. In this sense, clothing acts as a signifier;[29] in contrast, Goffman describes the nonverbal meaning of fashion as 'body gloss'.[30] Lurie[31] considers the significance of clothing and ornamentation, as defined by Flugel,[32] in terms of linguistic elements of codes, syntax and semantics as in all language. Solomon describes clothing styles and the fashions that influence them over time as codes which are dependent on context and interpretation.[33] In this sense, the interpretation of the particular code of particular clothing is a factor of the person wearing it, the occasion, the situation, who else is present and multiple other individual differences of the wearer and the perceiver as described previously. Solomon argues in terms of Eco's semiotics, claiming that the signified-signifier relationship is unstable in the context of clothing because the meanings associated with clothing items are influenced by many factors including taste, social identity and "access to the symbolic wares of a society".[34] Therefore, the meaning of what we wear needs to be interpreted in cultural, social and psychological terms. The idea of clothing or fashion as a language has been critiqued by Barnard, who claims that understanding clothing as language is problematic and ill-advised.[35] Although clothing, as a means of communication, may rely on a 'code', the code means different things to different people, and context must always be taken into account because clothing shown in the context of social interaction provides a broader range of information than typical studies in dress perception, which are context-free.[36] Others have critiqued the cultural meanings ascribed to clothing in fashion research as an artefact of a disproportionate focus on 'occasion wear' rather than on the realities of people's wardrobes; what they wear every day which is ordinary but varied, fluid and idiosyncratic. Accordingly, communicating personal information through clothing is complex and unsuitable for simple categorisation and stereotyping.

Additional problems associated with attempting to communicate through appearance only have been highlighted by several early researchers based on impression formation theory, developed by Asch.[37] Adopting a *Gestalt* framework, Asch investigated the way in which diverse elements of information are integrated into a general impression. Impression formation theory predicts that a general impression is a synthesised whole and, as such, more (Aristotle), or other (Koffka), than the sum of its parts. This concept is supported in research which demonstrates that the influence of a single appearance cue such as clothing on impression formation is affected by other appearance cues. However, much of this research has focused on individuals' impressions of strangers, rather than on impressions of familiar people. And others have found that clothing has little impact on interpersonal perceptions when the other person is familiar and when they are observed over time.

THE RECIPROCAL RELATIONSHIP OF BODY, MIND AND CLOTHING

We've all heard of the 'lucky' item of clothing or outfit. This is the item we wear when we really want something, and when we wear it, it gets us what we wish for. But of course, there's no such thing as a 'lucky' outfit. The 'luck' we experience is a result of many factors, including our behaviour, attitudes, experience and expectations and the behaviour, attitudes, experience and expectations of the person or people we are interacting with, as well as multiple factors from the specific situation. However, when all these factors work in our favour and the outcome is positive, we can convince ourselves that this was a result of wearing the 'lucky' item. This is another cognitive bias, in which heuristic thinking leads us to believe that a relationship exists between two unconnected events which happen simultaneously. Then we attribute cause and effect such that we believe the 'lucky' item caused the positive outcome. However, what might be happening is that we feel more confident because we are wearing the item, and this confidence is noticed by those we interact with, leading to an outcome that we were hoping for.

The interesting point is that we can imbue our clothing with symbolic meaning to influence how we feel and even, as we'll see later in this chapter, how we think. We can do this with any item, but, more interestingly, we can turn any piece of clothing into a 'lucky' item and use its symbolic power to help us feel confident (or whatever we want to feel). Early last century, psychologists attempted to understand the united role of body and mind in behaviour and emotion and, after much debate, concluded that physiological reactions and cognitive appraisal occur simultaneously. This has been supported by more recent research in cognitive appraisal theory which found that emotions can trigger physiological changes. Cognitive appraisal theory situates people's personal interpretations of an event in their emotional reaction. This finding is supported by neuroscience, which shows that the body helps us decide what to do in a particular situation. A basic claim of the embodiment framework is that all psychological processes are influenced by the body, while others claim that cognition exists for action which is situated in the environment and that it can occur without internal representations. Although the ideas of embodied cognition are convincing, they seem insufficient to bring about the paradigm shift that its proponents propose.[38] Nevertheless, relationships exist between the body, brain structures and concepts such as consciousness, emotion and self-awareness. The term *enclothed cognition*[39] was defined in a study extending the relationship between body and mind to the influence this can have on cognition.[40]

Enclothed cognition describes how clothing can influence cognitions by means of a phenomenon which depends on two factors occurring simultaneously: the symbolic meaning of the clothing and the actual wearing of the clothes. Adam and Galinsky argue that the experience of wearing clothes triggers associated abstract concepts and their symbolic meanings, causing the wearer to 'embody' the clothing and its symbolic meaning.[41] In doing so, the worn clothing influences the wearer's psychological processes by activating associated abstract concepts through its symbolic meaning. To test their hypothesis, Adam and Galinsky chose a white lab coat as the item of clothing and justified their choice as this item is worn by doctors and scientists. They suggested that the white lab coat's symbolism was its associative meaning of a scientific focus and emphasis on care and attention. This was verified by asking 38 people to rate the extent to which they associated the lab coat with attentiveness, carefulness, responsibility and a scientific focus on a scale from 1 (not at all) to 5 (very much).

In the first of their three experiments, they asked 58 participants to complete the Stroop Test (in which words for colours are presented in different colours; for example, the word *red* is written in blue). This test is used to measure selective attention, which is defined as the ability to focus on some stimuli while ignoring others. Half the participants performed the task in a white lab coat and were told that this was consistent with what previous participants had done; the others wore their own clothes. Interestingly, the participants wearing the lab coat made half as many errors. In the next experiment, participants were divided into three groups: one group wore the lab coat, which was described as a doctor's coat; another wore the lab coat, which was described as a painter's coat; and the third saw the lab coat on a desk but didn't wear it. All participants completed a 'spot the difference' task to measure their sustained attention. Participants wearing the lab coat described as a doctor's coat outperformed those in both the other groups. In the last study, the researchers allocated different participants to three groups: again one group wore the lab coat, described as a doctor's coat; another wore the lab coat, described as a painter's coat; and the third group was asked to write about the coat but not to wear it. All participants completed the spot the difference task. The researchers found that participants who wore the lab coat described as a doctor's coat performed best on the sustained attention task. The participants who wrote about how they identified with a lab coat performed second best, and those who wore the lab coat described as a painter's coat performed worst of all. Adam and Galinsky's study demonstrates the profound effect clothing can have on our cognitions.

SUMMARY

We have seen throughout the book that clothing is a powerful but ambiguous medium for expressing who we are. Perceiving colour is complex, yet wearing red or black makes us appear more attractive and sexier than people wearing other colours, but some people may interpret these colours as aggressive. Communicating meaning through clothing is complex and dependent on many factors, not least context. In addition to influencing mood, self-esteem and observers' impressions, clothing can also influence the wearer's cognitive abilities, as described by enclothed cognition.

7

CONCLUSIONS

Clearly, fashion matters beyond what our clothes say about us. Humans are involved in every aspect of fashion: design, production, manufacture, advertising and marketing, visual merchandising, retail, consumption and disposal. Fashion affects our self-perception and self-esteem, and although fashion is creative, exciting and dynamic, it has many problems. The intention of the psychology of fashion, as a discipline, is to go beyond understanding what our clothes say about us, to understanding human behaviour across the fashion industries and making a positive difference in the lives of its workers and its consumers as well as the environment in which we all live and work.

BRINGING IT ALL TOGETHER

Poor employment conditions, overconsumption and the very narrow stereotype of beauty promoted by the industry have ethical implications that until now have remained unchallenged. Psychologists can support professionals working in the fashion industry to promote a more inclusive and diverse representation of what is 'beautiful' through applying psychological science to understand these important problems and to predict and ultimately change behaviour.

This chapter recaps and integrates the main arguments posed throughout and considers what's next for the application of psychology to fashion. If you are reading this chapter after having read the book, you will have a better understanding of how fashion and behaviour are interrelated and how they influence each other and the world we live in. You may be motivated to find out more by engaging with the suggestions for further reading at the end of the book. You will know that multiple aspects of the clothes we wear and how we wear them matter at work and leisure. You may be excited by being more aware of the influence of social media on your wellbeing and mental health, and, as a consequence, you might interact with fashion and media imagery differently. You may also consider how fashion production and consumption are affecting the environment and choose to adopt a more sustainable approach to clothing.

Although fashion and cultural theorists talk of the 'meaning' of fashion, clothing or apparel, and how we interpret this meaning through appearance, they tend to do this from a non-psychological perspective. This is problematic in many ways, not least because perception, the interpretation of sensation to derive meaning, is a complex, subjective psychological process. There may be many reasons for the neglect of fashion by psychologists, but the tide is changing. The fashion industry is now aware of the role of human behaviour at the heart of their industry. A few universities and consultants are taking the opportunity to apply psychological knowledge to the context of fashion, not only to explain the notion of what our clothes say about us, but also to understand human behaviour across the industry, from sustainable practices to the psychological process of creativity.

We have discussed how fashion as a discipline is concerned with sensory perception, attention, memory, creativity and communication. As our second skin, fashion enables us to construct and express our identity. Fashion includes clothing, accessories, hairstyles and make-up; it is the vehicle by which we promote ourselves to others, and as such it involves reasoning, decision-making, problem-solving and social interaction. As a cultural phenomenon, fashion is concerned with meanings and symbols which provide instant visual communication. Even if we consider ourselves not interested in fashion, we all wear clothes. Fashion is inherently intertwined with human behaviour; therefore, fashion is psychology!

Over the past decades, interest in studying fashion has grown enormously. This is partly due to the rise in interest in consumer studies and the global economic importance of the fashion industry. The brief history of fashion provided in the introduction illustrated the long history of clothing for function and decoration, as a means of differentiation and belonging. It discussed the radical changes wrought by the Industrial Revolution. This discussion was brought up to date by considering the current concept of fashion as a cultural and social phenomenon, as exemplified in social groups and sub-cultures, which were further discussed in Chapter 4. Clearly, fashion is about more than frocks and frivolity. In agreement with Entwistle (2015), we have argued that the study of fashion breaches disciplinary boundaries. Fashion and cultural theorists have discussed, debated and critiqued many aspects of fashion. Many fashion theorists focus on the relationship between clothing and the body. However, the undeniable and inherent interrelationships between body and mind are often not discussed. It's as if they operated independently. However, fashion and cultural theorists have no difficulty in proposing the influence of fashion on identity and selfhood. What can be more psychological than these constructs? This book envisages fashion as so inherently concerned with human behaviour that it can be considered a form of psychology. One benefit of this is that psychology is a science; it looks beyond introspection, anecdote and intuition to evidence derived using scientific means. A scientific analysis of human behaviour can be used to understand and predict behaviour such that this knowledge can assist the fashion industry's response to the ethical and social problems it currently contributes to.

Mental health issues continue to be a growing problem globally. Rather than deal with the symptoms, the relatively new sub-discipline of psychology known as positive psychology, introduced in Chapter 2, deals with the causes. The growth of interest in this sub-discipline is related to the growth of interest in health and wellbeing that has developed over the past two decades. Psychological wellbeing is a component of positive psychology which describes how the ability to identify and use our character strengths contributes to our wellbeing. Moreover, our wellbeing can be enhanced further by living what Seligman calls the meaningful life, making a contribution to something bigger than we are.[1] One way we can achieve this through fashion is by thinking and behaving in ethical and responsible ways with regard to what we buy and how we discard our clothing. Responsible consumption was discussed in Chapter 5. As important in terms of ethical and social responsibility in fashion is the way the industry treats its workers. From fashion professionals who design and model fashion to those working in sweatshops, workers continue to be exposed to conditions that exacerbate mental health issues. Whether the fashion industry attracts those with existing mental health problems, or the fashion industry contributes to the development of them, they cannot be ignored. An unfortunately common mental health symptom experienced by individuals is disordered eating. This can have a varied aetiology, but evidence has found that those with low body satisfaction are more likely to develop eating disorders as well as other mental health problems such as anxiety and depression.

The current 'ideal' promoted in fashion and fashion media is harmful, as exposure to it is almost unavoidable. As fashion consumers, we relate to this ideal because, as social psychology tells us, we like to identify with those we aspire to. For this reason, the pernicious influence of fashion's unattainable ideal is harmful to individuals who compare themselves to it and to those who strive, unsuccessfully, to achieve it. Chapter 3 illustrated how body dissatisfaction is an issue throughout the lifespan for many women and increasingly for men. Fortunately, for many people, these feelings come and go, but when they persist and become distressing, they can become a mental health problem known as body dysmorphic disorder. For others, the current importance given to physical appearance and 'beauty' leads them to consider undergoing cosmetic interventions. The increase in interventions is alarming, not least because many practitioners are unregulated. This issue has been addressed in a 2017 report by the Nuffield Council on Bioethics which discusses issues involved in the supply of and demand for cosmetic interventions.[2] These include increased use of social media, celebrity culture, economic and social trends and a culture that values youthfulness. The report recommends improved ethical practice on both the demand and supply sides and calls on the Advertising Standards Authority, social media companies, Ofcom, the Equality and Human Rights Commission, the Department for Education and app stores to be more vigilant with regard to the content that passes through their jurisdiction. It further recommends that the Royal College of Surgeons leads in supporting high standards in cosmetic surgery.

Without doubt, the fashion and media industries influence interest in cosmetic interventions. We have presented evidence that reading fashion blogs leads to greater internalisation of the thin ideal and a greater tendency to consider cosmetic surgery in adolescent girls. For older women, the attraction is the myth of eternal youth that can be realised through cosmetic interventions as this will counter the inevitable disease of ageing that they have been programmed to fear. Evidence has shown that when older women experience appreciation of their ageing bodies and appearance, they are less likely to seek cosmetic interventions. Younger women and men may be more susceptible to the influences of fashion imagery because of their increased use of social networking sites. Perhaps as these media become used extensively by the older population, they too will be detrimentally influenced in terms of their body image. Social networking sites have enabled ordinary people to enter a world previously reserved for the privileged few. This notion encourages usage and, as a corollary, image-based social comparison. Although awareness-raising about these issues has been on many people's agendas over the past few years, little has changed in terms of outcomes. Psychologists can be called on to educate and support parents, carers and teachers in communicating wisely to children about self-perception and how attributes other than those which are appearance-based are more sustainable and ultimately more valuable. Psychologists can also support consumers in understanding how to navigate media imagery without internalising it and therefore avoid making negative comparisons. Psychologists can also collaborate with professionals in the fashion industry with the aim of improving the welfare of their consumers by embracing a more inclusive and realistic definition of beauty.

We cannot separate clothing from the socially and culturally constructed concepts of self and identity. These were the focus of Chapter 4. It discussed how we come to know ourselves through the process of socialisation and how this is instrumental in our self-concept. The meaning of fashion in terms of the self and identity pointed to the subjective motivation of self-knowledge and, ultimately, self-enhancement. These concepts were defined in terms of their role in self-esteem and self-awareness. Several theories were presented. Self-perception theory is concerned with attitude formation, which is based in part on imagining how others see and judge us. Social cognition theory describes how our behaviour results from complex interactions of cognitive, affective and biological outcomes with multifaceted environmental events. We manage this by categorising and stereotyping, assigning 'similar' people to the same social group. Social identity theory describes the dilemma present in the desire to conform while simultaneously being unique; it explains how our self is enhanced when we find belonging in social groups. Related to this is social comparison theory, which proposes that we are motivated to assess our status by comparing ourselves with others with the intended outcome of feeling better about ourselves. Consequently, upward social comparison may lead to negative feelings of inadequacy, whereas downward comparison can lead to positive feelings and enhanced self-evaluation. Self-discrepancy theory illustrates the discomfort experienced due to discrepancies between one's perceived actual and ideal self. Attribution theory describes how individuals are motivated to construct the meaning of and find the cause of a past event. We use information about another person's behaviour and its effects to draw a 'correspondent inference' in which the behaviour is attributed to a disposition or personality characteristic. These theories were then used to explain the role of fashion in self-identity and self-expression.

The current focus on sexualisation in music, film and fashion coupled with the increased availability of image-based content has contributed to the negative experience of objectification. Socialisation and experiences of sexual objectification can lead to mental health problems including body surveillance, body dissatisfaction, anxiety about appearance and eating disorders. Research suggests that diversifying the images of women in the mass media would help reduce the incidences of self-objectification and the associated negative outcomes. Unfortunately, this message seems to have escaped the notice of many professionals in the fashion industry who create and perpetuate the current ideal. Although there have been improvements recently, these have been described by some as tokenism as it is still the exception to see fashion imagery portraying disabled, older, Black or Asian individuals on the catwalk or elsewhere. A discussion of the influence of non-representation, misrepresentation and marginalisation of these populations was presented. Finally, in Chapter 4, the discussion moved to social groups and subcultures, dealing with the sense of belongingness we derive from our social groups and how fashion is an outward expression of the social groups and subcultures we belong to. Without doubt, the narrow stereotype of beauty promoted through fashion results in dissatisfaction for many minority groups. This is a major issue as researchers found that consumers like to see clothes on people who look like they do. Although there has been some improvement recently, it is still the exception to see disabled, older, Black or Asian models on the catwalk or in magazines, and the stereotype of 'beauty' is reinforced through the multibillion-dollar cosmetic industry.

Chapter 6 was concerned with fashion and behaviour and explained the reasons behind our fashion choices. Shopping is one of the most popular leisure pursuits, and as consumers we may believe that "to have is to be". Many differences exist with regard to shopping preferences. These may be demographic or psychographic, and each can contribute to the approach we take when shopping for fashion. This chapter briefly considered the rise of fitspiration and the increased use of athleisure wear as fashion. This led us into a discussion of conspicuous consumption, an idea that started at the end of the 19th century yet still has meaning today. Conspicuous consumption may underlie particular shopping behaviours such as impulsive and compulsive shopping. When compulsive shopping becomes obsessive, it is described as a mental health problem: compulsive buying disorder. This mental health issue typically starts in adolescence and affects women more than men (although this may be a matter of the degree of willingness to disclose on the part of men).

One of the many issues associated with the fast fashion industry is overconsumption. Recycling, reuse and upcycling are ways of reducing fashion and textile wastage, but individuals' attitudes to these vary. One reason for the variation is the symbolism, the psychological essentialism that is associated with the garment. On the positive side, fast fashion is an equaliser in that it permits ordinary fashion consumers to buy the latest fashion styles at an affordable price. However, consumers may get misled by the cheap price and not consider the quality of what they are buying. As a result, fast fashion items often have a short life before being discarded to landfill sites. Consumers may also be misled into believing that a higher price equals better quality or more ethical approaches to production, but, as noted, this is not always the case. To bring this chapter to a close, the discussion turned to two recent studies which demonstrate the power of clothing to enhance wellbeing. The time has come to move from raising awareness to making a positive difference. These dilemmas need to be resolved sooner than later if we are to improve wellbeing and reduce environmental damage. The professionals who can contribute to solving these important issues are psychologists, as they can design rigorous, evidence-based, iterative behaviour change interventions that begin to address these problems.

Early last century, evidence showed that people dress to please their own sex, to be modest and to enhance their physical features. A later study found that we choose our clothing to conform, maximise personal appearance and to express ourselves. Whatever our intentions, our clothing may communicate a different and unintended message and influence our behaviour, our mood and even our cognitions.

Colour is an important feature of fashion, but the colour we perceive is a factor of many physical and psychological processes. This was illustrated with the example of 'the dress', which caused a stir on social media in 2014. The colours red and black have received considerably more attention than other colours in research on clothing and appearance. Findings from some of the studies that have investigated the influence of these colours was presented, followed by discussion of the little black dress before moving on to the topic of clothing in the workplace. Some proponents, including Eco and Lurie,[3] claim that clothing communicates through a process akin to spoken or written language. They describe fashion as a code with syntax and semantics. However, this view neglects the need to interpret clothing in cultural, social and psychological terms. Evidence regarding interpretations of individuals' characteristics and so on are often based on artificial stimuli: images of strangers. In reality, context and individual differences cannot be ignored in interpreting appearance. Moreover, we are likely to change our interpretations over time as we get to know the person. We saw previously that clothing can be imbued with symbolic meaning to enhance the relationship the wearer has with the item and, ultimately, improve their subjective wellbeing. However, recent research has found that clothing can also enhance the wearer's cognitive abilities. This was the focus of the final section of Chapter 6, in which the concepts of embodied cognition and enclothed cognition were presented. Enclothed cognition proposes that clothes can influence cognitions dependent on two factors occurring simultaneously: the symbolic meaning of the clothing and the actual wearing of the clothes. Adam and Galinsky's study[4] demonstrated the power of the wearer to exploit clothing and fashion as a vehicle for positive change and empowerment.

WHAT'S NEXT?

Human lives are changing. One third of the people born in the next decade will live to be 100 years old and older. How will the fashion industry respond?

Fashion is defined by novelty and change. The relentless pace of fashion has been cited as contributing to professionals burning out. Fashion weeks traditionally show collections one season in advance, but this may be changing. Diane Von Furstenberg, Chair of the Council of Fashion Designers of America, announced plans to become more consumer facing: collections will be available to buy immediately. Soon after this announcement, Burberry, Tom Ford and Tommy Hilfiger announced similar plans. Whether this is a move to address consumers' desire to see now, have now, or a ploy by brands to exploit consumers' excitement at seeing new collections, is unknown, but certainly fashion companies are adopting technology to boost sales as a result of competition from companies such as Amazon. Some brands have used technology to enhance the appearance of their designs, and some have used it to enable communication via social media. For example, Cute Circuit's gorgeous creations use fabrics with circuitry and sensing capabilities woven into their fibres. These designs are aesthetically pleasing, but the additional benefits of applying technological innovation to fashion, such as health and wellbeing, are yet to be realised on a large scale.

Consumers are becoming more knowledgeable and more demanding. Fashion consumers in the 21st century use multiple channels to compare prices and delivery options and select the most appropriate one for their needs at the time. The ability to return unwanted items is seen as a requirement for consumers but a problem for companies, and much of what is returned is not resold. The competition among retailers is tough, and if companies are to remain viable, they need to address their consumers' needs. Consumer experience is a hot topic. Consumers of luxury fashion are accustomed to personalised service, but high street shoppers are just beginning to see this. Sephora, a global store which sells make-up, has just opened a 'local' store in a Boston neighbourhood to encourage consumers who prefer to shop locally. The rationale behind the decision to open Sephora Studio is that people have less time to visit out-of-town malls. Sephora Studio uses the same interior branding but has far less stock. Instead, it has highly trained staff equipped with electronic tablets that enable them to find the items their customers want if they're not in the Studio. Customers order and make purchases via the tablets. Items they want that aren't instore can be delivered within hours. Sephora Studio considers a positive consumer experience essential to customer loyalty. This attitude is shared by many brands as they are beginning to understand that if a consumer gets poor service, he or she is unlikely to stay in the store or to return. In addition, poor service is likely to result in poor feedback. Consumers take reviews of products and services seriously; therefore, it is in the interest of the company or brand concerned to ensure they give the best service and get the best feedback.

Augmented reality (AR) and virtual reality (VR) are technologies that have been around for decades but have been a long time coming to fashion. By the time this book is published, it is likely that VR simulations of store environments will exist. In a few years, they will be commonplace. Tommy Hilfiger and Coach already have VR headsets in their stores to allow their customers to experience their label's fashion show. Gap has introduced an AR dressing room that allows consumers to try its ranges digitally. However, this works only with a specific smartphone. An obvious application for AR is beauty. According to a recent report by the Business of Fashion, several brands, including Sephora, Charlotte Tilbury and Rimmel, have been early adopters of AR systems that allow their consumers to 'try on' cosmetics via their phones.[5] Research has shown that AR applications can boost sales by up to 22%, but an even more valuable benefit is the data that AR or VR can collect. Having smart mirrors in fitting rooms would be a smart idea. Research has shown that we are far less likely to make a purchase if we need to get dressed and find a different size to try on. A smart mirror, or even a tablet, could be installed in fitting rooms to allow the customer to see herself via an AR application, to order the next size up (or down) or to browse and order accessories that would complement the item she or he wishes to purchase.

Bespoke pieces could have a microchip embedded that tells the story of the creation of the garment. This would encourage consumers to appreciate the craft that has created the item and the legacy of the brand behind it. As technology becomes cheaper, it might be possible to embed similar technology into mass-produced items to encourage wearers to engage with the item and keep it longer. This might even be a way to imbue an item with symbolic meaning as described previously in this book.

Furthermore, tech companies are working with fashion brands: for example, Google and Levi's, and Intel and Hussein Chalayan. The use of 3D printing is growing, and sewbots could be the future of fashion production. Technology-enhanced clothing could address some of the more pressing problems in fashion such as sustainability. For example, biotech is producing new materials that are grown in the lab from resources such as collagen. These could reduce the demand for natural resources and wastage as whole garments could be manufactured as opposed to manufacturing fabrics that need to be cut into the component parts of a clothing item. Material scientists will develop materials embedded with optical fibres or yet-to-be designed technologies that are sustainable not only in terms of saving natural resources but also in terms of their durability. They will be flexible and lightweight, will adjust according to the wearer's body temperature and will be biodegradable. Furthermore, they will not harm the environment when laundered.

What might future careers in fashion look like? Of course, there will still be editors, designers, buyers, stylists and photographers. However, as the demand for fashion-tech accelerates, new careers in fashion are being created. These are likely to include biologists, who will develop exciting new fabrics and textiles grown in labs; materials scientists, who will develop smart materials that enhance the wearer's wellbeing as well as enabling data about them to be collected; specialists in 3D printing, who will assist in the design and manufacturing processes; data scientists, who will analyse and interpret the billions of data points collected on consumers; environmentalists, who will support the industry move to more ethical and socially responsible practices; and of course psychologists, who will work with all professionals working in the fashion industry, using their knowledge and skills to understand human behaviour and enhance wellbeing at the individual, societal and global levels. Consumer psychologists will become even more necessary as consumers demand meaningful shopping experiences. Psychologists who are able to contribute to multidisciplinary teams with a rich understanding of human behaviour *and* fashion will be sought by educators and industry. Psychology and fashion are now engaged; let's celebrate their future marriage. May they live happily ever after.

FURTHER READING

Anguelov, N. (2015). *The dirty side of the garment industry: Fast fashion and its negative impact on environment and society.* Boca Raton, FL: Taylor Frances.

Barnard, M. (2002). *Fashion as communication.* Hove, UK: Psychology Press.

Bruce, V., Green, P. R., & Georgeson, M. A. (2003). *Visual perception: Physiology, psychology, & ecology.* Hove, UK: Psychology Press.

Bull, R., & Rumsey, N. (2012). *The social psychology of facial appearance.* Berlin: Springer Science & Business Media.

Cash, T. F., & Pruzinsky, T. (2004). *Body image: A handbook of theory, research, and clinical practice.* New York: Guilford Press.

Coolican, H. (2014). *Research methods and statistics in psychology.* London: Hodder & Stoughton Educational.

Cosgrave, B. (2001). *The complete history of costume & fashion: From ancient Egypt to the present day.* New York: Checkmark Books.

Davis, F. (1985). Clothing and fashion as communication. In *The psychology of fashion* (pp. 15–27). Lexington, MA: Lexington Books.

Davis, F. (1994). *Fashion, culture, and identity.* Chicago, IL: University of Chicago Press.

Entwistle, J. (2015). *The fashioned body: Fashion, dress and social theory.* Hoboken, NJ: John Wiley & Sons.

Eysenck, M. W., & Keane, M. T. (2000). *Cognitive psychology: A student's handbook.* New York: Taylor & Francis.

Gelman, S. A. (2013). Artifacts and essentialism. *Review of Philosophy and Psychology, 4*(3), 449–463.

Grogan S. (2008). *Body image: Understanding body dissatisfaction in men, women, and children.* London/New York: Routledge.

Hefferon, K. (2013). *Positive psychology and the body: The somatopsychic side to flourishing.* New York: McGraw-Hill Education.

Heti, S., Julavits, H., & Shapton, L. (2014). *Women in clothes.* London: Penguin.

Hoskins, T. E. (2014). *Stitched up: The anti-capitalist book of fashion.* London: Pluto Press.

Jarrett, C. (2014). *Great myths of the brain.* Hoboken, NJ: John Wiley & Sons.

Kohrer, E., & Schaffrin, M. (2016). *Fashion made fair: Modern-innovative-sustainable.* London: Prestel Publishing.

McDougall, W. (2015). *An introduction to social psychology.* Hove, UK: Psychology Press.

Nuffield Council on Bioethics. (2017). *Cosmetic procedures: Ethical issues.* http://nuf fieldbioethics.org/wp-content/uploads/Cosmetic-procedures-full-report.pdf

Peterson, C., & Seligman, M. E. (2004). *Character strengths and virtues: A handbook and classification* (Vol. 1). Oxford: Oxford University Press.

Pruzinsky, T., & Cash, T. F. (Eds.) (2002). *Body image: A handbook of theory, research, and clinical practice.* New York: Guilford Press.

Rocamora, A. (2015). *Thinking through fashion: A guide to key theorists.* New York: IB Tauris.

Sedikides, C., & Brewer, M. B. (Eds.) (2015). *Individual self, relational self, collective self.* Hove, UK: Psychology Press.

Seligman, M. E. (2017). *Authentic happiness: Using the new positive psychology to realize your potential for lasting fulfillment.* Boston: Nicholas Brealey Publishing.

Shapiro, L. (2010). *Embodied cognition.* New York: Routledge.

Snyder, C. R., & Lopez, S. J. (Eds.) (2009). *Oxford handbook of positive psychology.* Oxford: Oxford University Press.

Solomon, M. R. (2017). *Consumer behavior: Buying, having, and being, global.* London: Pearson Education Ltd.

Solomon, M. R., & Rabolt, N. J. (2004). *Consumer behavior: In fashion.* Upper Saddle River, NJ: Prentice Hall.

Steele, V. (Ed.) (2004). *Fashion theory: The journal of dress, body & culture.* Oxford: Berg.

Stoyanov, S. (2017). *A theory of human motivation.* Boca Raton, FL: CRC Press.

Tajfel, H. (1981). *Human groups and social categories: Studies in social psychology.* Cambridge University Press Archive.

Tamagni, D. (2015). *Fashion tribes: Global street style*. New York: Harry N. Abrams, Inc.

Tedeschi, J. T. (Ed.) (2013). *Impression management theory and social psychological research*. Cambridge, MA: Academic Press.

Wolf, N. (1991). *The beauty myth: How images of women are used against women*. London: Vintage.

NOTES

CHAPTER 1

1 *Oxford English Dictionary.* https://en.oxforddictionaries.com/definition/psychology

2 British Psychological Society. www.bps.org.uk/what-we-do/bps/bps

3 American Psychological Association. www.apa.org/support/about-apa.aspx

4 *Oxford English Dictionary.* https://en.oxforddictionaries.com/definition/fashion

5 www.tandfonline.com/action/journalInformation?show=aimsScope&journalCode=rfft20

6 Hoskins, T. E. (2014). *Stitched up: The anti-capitalist book of fashion.* London: Pluto Press, p. 4.

7 Barnard, M. (2002). *Fashion as communication.* Hove, UK: Psychology Press.

8 Fashion United. Global fashion industry statistics – international apparel. https://fashionunited.com/global-fashion-industry-statistics

9 Kaiser, S. B. (1997). *The social psychology of clothing* (rev. ed.). New York: Fairchild.

10 Veblen, T. (1899). *The theory of the leisure class: An economic study in the evolution of institutions.* New York: Macmillan.

11 Amed, I., Berg, A., Brantberg, L., & Hedrich, S. (2016). *The state of fashion.* Business of Fashion and McKinsey & Company. www.mckinsey.com/industries/retail/our-insights/the-state-of-fashion

CHAPTER 2

1 Seligman, M. E., & Csikszentmihalyi, M. (2014). Positive psychology: An introduction. In Flow and the foundations of positive psychology (pp. 279–298). Dordrecht: Springer Netherlands, p. 279.

2 Stoyanov, S. (2017). A theory of human motivation. Boca Raton, FL: CRC Press.

3 The Pursuit of Happiness. Martin Seligman. www.pursuit-of-happiness.org/history-of-happiness/martin-seligman-psychology

4 Mental Health Foundation. (2016, September 29). Adult psychiatric morbity survey: Survey of mental health and wellbeing, England, 2014. http://content.digital.nhs.uk/catalogue/PUB21748

5 World Health Organization. (2011, December 1). Global burden of mental disorders and the need for a comprehensive, coordinated response from health and social sectors at the country level. http://apps.who.int/gb/ebwha/pdf_files/EB130/B130_9-en.pdf

6 Mental Health Foundation. (2016, September 29). Adult psychiatric morbity survey: Survey of mental health and wellbeing, England, 2014. http://content.digital.nhs.uk/catalogue/PUB21748

7 Fitzsimmons-Craft, E. E. (2011). Social psychological theories of disordered eating in college women: Review and integration. Clinical Psychology Review, 31(7), 1224–1237.

8 Festinger, L. (1954). A theory of social comparison processes. Human Relations, 7(2), 117–140.

9 Blumler, J. G., Brown, J. R., & McQuail, D. (1970). The social origins of the gratifications associated with television viewing. The British Social Science Research Council, UK.

10 Fredrickson, B. L., & Roberts, T. A. (1997). Objectification theory: Toward understanding women's lived experiences and mental health risks. Psychology of Women Quarterly, 21(2), 173–206.

11 The British Psychological Society. (2017, January 9). BPS response to Theresa May's speech on mental health. https://beta.bps.org.uk/news-and-policy/bps-response-theresa-mays-speech-mental-health

12 Nelson, B., & Rawlins, D. (2008). Relating schizotypy and personality to the phenomenology of creativity. Schizophrenia Bulletin, 36(2), 388–399.

13 Bellis, M. A., Hughes, K., Morleo, M., Tocque, K., Hughes, S., Allen, T., . . . & Fe-Rodriguez, E. (2007). Predictors of risky alcohol consumption in schoolchildren and their implications for preventing alcohol-related harm. Substance Abuse Treatment, Prevention, and Policy, 2(1), 15.

14 British Fashion Council. (2007). Model health inquiry report. www.britishfashioncouncil.co.uk/uploads/files/1/The%20Report%20of%20the%20Model%20Health%20Inquiry,%20September%202007.pdf

CHAPTER 3

1 Schilder, Paul. (1935). *The image and appearance of the human body: Studies in the constructive energies of the human psyche.* London: Kegan Paul, Trench, Trubner.

2 Grogan, S. (2008). *Body image: Understanding body dissatisfaction in men, women, and children.* New York: Routledge.

3 Wolf, N. (1991). *The beauty myth: How images of women are used against women.* London: Vintage.

4 The Children's Society. (2017). *Good childhood report.* www.childrenssociety.org. uk/sites/default/files/the-good-childhood-report-2017_full-report_0.pdf

5 Frederick, D. A., Sandhu, G., Morse, P. J., & Swami, V. (2016). Correlates of appearance and weight satisfaction in a US national sample: Personality, attachment style, television viewing, self-esteem, and life satisfaction. *Body Image, 17,* 191–203.

6 Mitchison, D., Hay, P., Griffiths, S., Murray, S. B., Bentley, C., Gratwick-Sarll, K., Harrison, C., & Mond, J. (2017). Disentangling body image: The relative associations of overvaluation, dissatisfaction, and preoccupation with psychological distress and eating disorder behaviors in male and female adolescents. *International Journal of Eating Disorders, 50,* 118–126. doi:10.1002/eat.22592

7 Sylvia, Z., King, T. K., & Morse, B. J. (2014). Virtual ideals: The effect of video game play on male body image. *Computers in Human Behavior, 37,* 183–188.

8 Swami, V. (2009). Body appreciation, media influence, and weight status predict consideration of cosmetic surgery among female undergraduates. *Body Image, 6*(4), 315–317.

9 Honigman, R. J., Phillips, K. A., & Castle, D. J. (2004). A review of psychosocial outcomes for patients seeking cosmetic surgery. *Plastic and Reconstructive Surgery, 113*(4), 1229.

10 American Society for Aesthetic Plastic Surgery. (2016). *Cosmetic surgery national data bank statistics.* www.surgery.org/sites/default/files/ASAPS-Stats2016.pdf

11 Ibid.

12 British Association of Aesthetic Plastic Surgeons. (2016, February 8). SUPER CUTS 'Daddy makeovers' and celeb confessions: Cosmetic surgery procedures soar in Britain. https://baaps.org.uk/about/news/38/super_cuts_daddy_makeovers_and_celeb_confessions_cosmetic_surgery_procedures_soar_in_britain

13 Nuffield Council on Bioethics. (2018). *Cosmetic procedures: Ethical issues.* https://nuffieldbioethics.org/project/cosmetic-procedures

14 Frederick, D. A., Lever, J., & Peplau, L. A. (2007). Interest in cosmetic surgery and body image: Views of men and women across the lifespan. *Plastic and Reconstructive Surgery, 120*(5), 1407–1415.

15 Mair, C., Wade, G., & Tamburic, S. (2015). Older women want to look good despite media pressure to look young. *International Journal of Aging and Society*, 5(1), 1–10.

16 Tiggemann, M. (2015). Considerations of positive body image across various social identities and special populations. *Body Image*, 14, 168–176.

17 Cili, S., Mair, C., & Kljakovic, M. (under review). The influence of advertising for cosmetics on middle-aged and older women: An online survey. *Aging and Society*.

18 Garland-Thomson, R. (2002). Integrating disability, transforming feminist theory. *NWSA Journal*, 14(3), 1–32, 12.

19 Changing Faces. (2017). *Disfigurement in the UK*. www.changingfaces.org.uk/wp-content/uploads/2017/05/DITUK.pdf

20 Changing Faces. (2017). *About disfigurement*. www.changingfaces.org.uk/campaigns/dituk/about-disfigurement

21 Wolf, N. (1991). *The beauty myth: How images of women are used against women*. London: Vintage.

22 Leppänen, S., Westinen, E., & Kytola, S. (Eds.) (2016). *Social media discourse, (dis)identifications and diversities*. New York and London: Taylor & Francis.

23 Statista. Internet statistics and market data about the Internet. www.statista.com/markets/424/internet/

24 Statista. Leading fashion brands ranked by number of Instagram followers as of August 2017 (in millions). www.statista.com/statistics/483738/leading-fashion-brands-instagram-followers/

25 For the cover, see www.vogue.com/article/supermodel-cover-september-2014.

26 Harris, S. (2017, March 11). What is an influencer? *Vogue*. www.vogue.co.uk/article/what-is-an-influencer

27 Ibid.

28 Best, P., Manktelow, R., & Taylor, B. (2014). Online communication, social media and adolescent wellbeing: A systematic narrative review. *Children and Youth Services Review*, 41, 27–36.

29 Changing Faces. (2017, June 12). New government 'must act' on social media abuse. www.changingfaces.org.uk/new-government-must-act-social-media-abuse

30 Ousley, L., Cordero, E., & White, S. (2008). Fat talk among college students: How undergraduates communicate regarding food and body weight, shape and appearance. *Eating Disorders*, 16(1), 73–84.

31 Johnson, K., Lennon, S. J., & Rudd, N. (2014). Dress, body and self: Research in the social psychology of dress. *Fashion and Textiles*, 1(1), 20.

32 Salk, R. H., & Engeln-Maddox, R. (2011). "If you're fat, then I'm humongous!" Frequency, content, and impact of fat talk among college women. *Psychology of Women Quarterly*, 35(1), 18–28.

33 Sladek, M., Engeln, R., & Miller, S. (2014). Development and validation of the male body talk scale: A psychometric investigation. *Body Image*, 11(3), 233–244.

34 Rudiger, J. A., & Winstead, B. A. (2013). Body talk and body-related co-rumination: Associations with body image, eating attitudes, and psychological adjustment. *Body Image*, 10(4), 462–471.

35 Fredrickson, B. L., & Roberts, T. A. (1997). Objectification theory: Toward understanding women's lived experiences and mental health risks. *Psychology of Women Quarterly*, 21(2), 173–206.

36 Fredrickson, B. L., & Roberts, T. A. (1997). Objectification theory: Toward understanding women's lived experiences and mental health risks. *Psychology of Women Quarterly*, 21(2), 173–206.

37 Tylka, T. L. (2004). The relation between body dissatisfaction and eating disorder symptomatology: An analysis of moderating variables. *Journal of Counseling Psychology*, 51(2), 178.

38 Fredrickson, B. L., & Roberts, T. A. (1997). Objectification theory: Toward understanding women's lived experiences and mental health risks. *Psychology of Women Quarterly*, 21(2), 173–206.

39 Fredrickson, B. L., Roberts, T. A., Noll, S. M., Quinn, D. M., & Twenge, J. M. (1998). That swimsuit becomes you: Sex differences in self-objectification, restrained eating, and math performance. *Journal of Personality and Social Psychology*, 75(1), 269–284.

40 Martins, Y., Tiggemann, M., & Kirkbride, A. (2007). Those Speedos become them: The role of self-objectification in gay and heterosexual men's body image. *Personality and Social Psychology Bulletin*, 33(5), 634–647.

41 Roberts, T. A., & Gettman, J. Y. (2004). Mere exposure: Gender differences in the negative effects of priming a state of self-objectification. *Sex Roles*, 51(1), 17–27.

42 McKinley, N. M. (1998). Gender differences in undergraduates' body esteem: The mediating effect of objectified body consciousness and actual/ideal weight discrepancy. *Sex Roles*, 39(1), 113–123.

CHAPTER 4

1 James, W. (1890). *The principles of psychology* (Vol. 1). London: Palgrave Macmillan, p. 21.

2 Maslow, A. H. (1943). A theory of human motivation. *Psychological Review*, 50(4), 370.

3 Maslow, A. H. (1969). Various meanings of transcendence. *The Journal of Transpersonal Psychology*, 1(1), 55–56.

4 Creekmore, A. M. (1963). *Clothing behaviors and their relation to general values and to the striving for basic needs* (Doctoral dissertation, Pennsylvania State University).

5 Hixon, J. G., & Swann, W. B. (1993). When does introspection bear fruit? Self-reflection, self-insight, and interpersonal choices. *Journal of Personality and Social Psychology*, 64(1), 35.

6 Bem, D. J. (1972). Self-perception theory. *Advances in Experimental Social Psychology*, 6, 1–62.

7 Kellerman, J. M., & Laird, J. D. (1982). The effect of appearance on self-perceptions. *Journal of Personality*, 50(3), 296–351.

8 Kwon, Y. (1994). The influence of appropriateness of dress and gender on the self-perception of occupational attributes. *Clothing and Textile Research Journal*, 12(3), 33–39.

9 Peluchette, J., & Karl, K. (2007). The impact of workplace attire on employee self-perceptions. *Human Resource Development Quarterly*, 18(3), 345–360.

10 Guy, A., & Banim, M. (2000). Personal collections: Women's clothing use and identity. *Journal of Gender Studies*, 9(3), 313–327.

11 Ibid., p. 321.

12 Bandura, A. (1969). Social-learning theory of identificatory processes. *Handbook of Socialization Theory and Research*, 213, 262.

13 Festinger, L. (1954). A theory of social comparison processes. *Human Relations*, 7(2), 117–140.

14 Morse, S., & Gergen, K. J. (1970). Social comparison, self-consistency, and the concept of self. *Journal of Personality and Social Psychology*, 16(1), 148.

15 Higgins, E. T. (1987). Self-discrepancy: A theory relating self and affect. *Psychological Review*, 94(3), 319.

16 Tajfel, H. (Ed.) (2010). *Social identity and intergroup relations*. Cambridge: Cambridge University Press.

17 Wilson, E. (1985). *Adorned in dreams: Fashion and modernity*. London: Virago.

18 Kaiser, S. B., & Freeman, C. M. (1989, August). Meaningful clothing and the framing of emotion: Toward a gender-relational understanding. Paper presented at the meeting of the Society for the Study of Symbolic Interaction, San Francisco.

19 Lewis, D. C., Medvedev, K., & Seponski, D. M. (2011). Awakening to the desires of older women: Deconstructing ageism within fashion magazines. *Journal of Aging Studies*, 25(2), 101–109.

20 Hunter, M. L. (2011). Buying racial capital: Skin-bleaching and cosmetic surgery in a globalized world. *Journal of Pan African Studies*, 4(4), 142–149.

21 Kang, J., & Park-Poaps, H. (2011). Motivational antecedents of social shopping for fashion and its contribution to shopping satisfaction. *Clothing and Textiles Research Journal*, 29(4), 331–347.

22 Wasylkiw, L., Emms, A. A., Meuse, R., & Poirier, K. F. (2009). Are all models created equal? A content analysis of women in advertisements of fitness versus fashion magazines. *Body Image*, 6(2), 137–140.

23 Lewis, D. C., Medvedev, K., & Seponski, D. M. (2011). Awakening to the desires of older women: Deconstructing ageism within fashion magazines. *Journal of Aging Studies*, 25(2), 101–109.

24 Burns, J. (2013, August 15). Few over-65s feel old but half object to ageism – survey. *BBC News*. www.bbc.co.uk/news/education-23697349

25 Jones, H. (2015, June 22). The economics of retirement: The power of pensioner spending. *The Guardian*. www.theguardian.com/money/2015/jun/22/economics-of-retirement-power-pensioner-spending

26 Scope. (2017, March). Disability facts and figures. *Family Resources Survey: Financial Year 2015/16*. www.scope.org.uk/media/disability-facts-figures #La6SUCvaBM6v0qGG.99

27 Garland-Thomson, R. (2002). Integrating disability, transforming feminist theory. *NWSA Journal*, 14(3), 1–32.

28 Garland-Thomson, R. (2002). Integrating disability, transforming feminist theory. *NWSA Journal*, 14(3), 1–32.

29 (2017, July 17). The fashion industry pays attention to plus-size women. *The Economist*. https://www.economist.com/news/business/21725029-revenue-category-outstripping-total-clothing-sales-fashion-industry-pays

30 Campbell, D. T. (1958). Common fate, similarity, and other indices of the status of aggregates of persons as social entities. *Systems Research and Behavioral Science*, 3(1), 14–25.

31 Campbell, D. T. (1958). Common fate, similarity, and other indices of the status of aggregates of person as social entities. *Behavioural Science*, 3, 14–25.

CHAPTER 5

1 News Agencies. (2013, September 16). Vivienne Westwood: Everyone buys too many clothes. *Telegraph*. http://fashion.telegraph.co.uk/news-features/TMG10312077/Vivienne-Westwood-Everyone-buys-too-many-clothes.html

2 Willis, A., and agencies. (2013, July 5). Average male gets bored on shopping trip after just 26 minutes. *Telegraph*. www.telegraph.co.uk/news/uknews/10161610/Average-male-gets-bored-on-shopping-trip-after-just-26-minutes.html

3 Tiggemann, M., & Zaccardo, M. (2015). "Exercise to be fit, not skinny": The effect of fitspiration imagery on women's body image. *Body Image*, 15, 61–67.

4 McCracken, G. D., & Roth, V. J. (1989). Does clothing have a code? Empirical findings and theoretical implications in the study of clothing as a means of communication. *International Journal of Research in Marketing*, 6(1), 13–33.

5 Veblen, T. (1899). *Theory of the leisure class: An economic study in the evolution of institutions*.

6 Solomon, M. R., & Rabolt, N. J. (2004). *Consumer behavior: In fashion*. Upper Saddle River, NJ: Prentice Hall.

7 Black, D. W. (2007). A review of compulsive buying disorder. *World Psychiatry*, 6(1), 14–18.

8 Koran, L. M., Faber, R. J., Aboujaoude, E., Large, M. D., & Serpe, R. T. (2006). Estimated prevalence of compulsive buying behavior in the United States. *American Journal of Psychiatry*, 163(10), 1806–1812.

9 McElroy, S. L., Satlin, A., Pope, H. G., Keck, P. E., & Hudson, J. I. (1991). Treatment of compulsive shopping with antidepressants: A report of three cases. *Annals of Clinical Psychiatry*, 3(3), 199–204.

10 Black, D. W. (2007). A review of compulsive buying disorder. *World Psychiatry*, 6(1), 14.

11 Hood, B. (2016). Make recycled goods covetable: To reduce consumption and waste we must overcome our squeamishness about repurposing pre-owned possessions. *Nature*, 531(7595), 438–441.

12 Hood, B. M., & Bloom, P. (2008). Children prefer certain individuals over perfect duplicates. *Cognition*, 106, 455–462.

13 Meyer, M., Leslie, S. J., Gelman, S. A., & Stilwell, S. M. (2013). Essentialist beliefs about bodily transplants in the United States and India. *Cognitive Science*, 37(4), 668–710.

14 Clean Clothes Campaign. (2015, January 23). Clean Clothes Campaign contribution to the informal meeting with stakeholders on responsible

management of the supply chain in the garment sector. European Commission, Brussels. cleanclothes.org/img/pdf/ccc-contribution-flagship-initiative

15 2015 Annual Report. (2016, March 10). https://cleanclothes.org/about/annual-reports/2015-annual-report/view. Clean Clothes Campaign. (2014). Stitched up: Poverty wages for garment workers in Eastern Europe and Turkey. https://cleanclothes.org/livingwage/stitched-up. Luginbühl, C. (2017). *Labour on a shoestring*. https://cleanclothes.org/resources/recommended-reading/labour-on-a-shoestring

16 Friedman, V. (2017, April 20). The new meaning of fast fashion. *The New York Times*. www.nytimes.com/2017/04/20/fashion/farfetch-gucci-designer-delivery.html?mwrsm=Email&_r=0

17 Fleetwood-Smith, R. & Hefferon, K. (2015). Attachment theory applied to clothing. British Psychological Society Annual Conference, Liverpool UK, 5–7 May.

18 Fleetwood-Smith, R., Hefferon, K., and Mair, C. (under review). Personal enclothed cognition: Understanding the symbolic experience of actively worn attachment clothing. *International Journal of Fashion Studies*.

19 Adam, H., & Galinsky, A. D. (2012). Enclothed cognition. *Journal of Experimental Social Psychology*, 48(4), 918–925.

20 Fleetwood-Smith, R., Hefferon, K., and Mair, C. (under review). Personal enclothed cognition: Understanding the symbolic experience of actively worn attachment clothing. *International Journal of Fashion Studies*.

21 Shaughnessey, Z. (2017). The lived experience of female breast cancer survivors, and their relationship with clothing, from a posttraumatic growth perspective. British Psychological Society Annual Conference, Brighton UK, 3–5 May.

CHAPTER 6

1 Simmel, G. (1957). Fashion. *American Journal of Sociology*, 62(6), 541–558, 542.

2 Ibid., p. 544.

3 Bourdieu, P. (1984). *Distinction: A social critique of the judgement of taste*. Cambridge, MA: Harvard University Press.

4 Hurlock, E. B. (1929). The psychology of dress: An analysis of fashion and its motive. *International Quarterly*, 10(1904), 130–155.

5 Barr, E. D. Y. (1934). *A psychological analysis of fashion motivation* (Vol. 26, No. 171–178). New York: Columbia University.

6 Asch, S. E. (1964). The process of free recall. In C. Scheerer (Ed.), *Cognition: theory, research, promise* (pp. 79–88). New York: Harper & Row. Milgram, S.

(1963). Behavioral study of obedience. *Journal of Abnormal and Social Psychology*, 67(4), 371. Haney, C., Banks, W. C., & Zimbardo, P. G. (1973). A study of prisoners and guards in a simulated prison. *Naval Research Reviews*, 9, 1–17.

7 Bellezza, S., Gino, F., & Keinan, A. The red sneakers effect: Inferring status and competence from signals of nonconformity. *Journal of Consumer Research*, 41(1), 35–54.

8 Damhorst, M. L. (1990). In search of a common thread: Classification of information communicated through dress. *Clothing and Textiles Research Journal*, 8(2), 1–12.

9 Behling, D. U., & Williams, E. A. (1991). Influence of dress on perception of intelligence and expectations of scholastic achievement. *Clothing and Textiles Research Journal*, 9(4), 1–7.

10 Cahoon, D. D., & Edmonds, E. M. (1989). Male-female estimates of opposite-sex first impressions concerning females' clothing styles. *Bulletin of the Psychonomic Society*, 27(3), 280–281.

11 Johnson, K. K., & Workman, J. E. (1992). Clothing and attributions concerning sexual harassment. *Family and Consumer Sciences Research Journal*, 21(2), 160–172.

12 Moody, W., Kinderman, P., & Sinha, P. (2010). An exploratory study: Relationships between trying on clothing, mood, emotion, personality and clothing preference. *Journal of Fashion Marketing and Management: An International Journal*, 14(1), 161–179.

13 Bramley, E. V. (2017, February 3). Dopamine dressing – can you dress yourself happy? *Guardian*. www.theguardian.com/fashion/2017/feb/03/dopamine-dressing-can-you-dress-yourself-happy

14 Schlaffke, L., Golisch, A., Haag, L., Lenz, M., Heba, S., Lissek, S., . . ., Tegenthoff, M. (2015). The brain's dress code: How the Dress allows to decode the neuronal pathway of an optical illusion. *Cortex*, 73, 271–275.

15 Elliot, A. J. (2015). Color and psychological functioning: A review of theoretical and empirical work. *Frontiers in Psychology*, 6.

16 Goethe, J. W. V. (1840). *Theory of colours*. 1810. Trans. by Charles Lock Eastlake. London: John Murray, Albemarle Street.

17 Pazda, A. D., Elliot, A. J., & Greitemeyer, T. (2012). Sexy red: Perceived sexual receptivity mediates the red-attraction relation in men viewing woman. *Journal of Experimental Social Psychology*, 48(3), 787–790.

18 Roberts, S. C., Owen, R. C., & Havlicek, J. (2010). Distinguishing between perceiver and wearer effects in clothing color-associated attributions. *Evolutionary Psychology*, 8(3), 350–364.

19 Feltman, R., & Elliot, A. J. (2011). The influence of red on perceptions of relative dominance and threat in a competitive context. *Journal of Sport and Exercise Psychology, 33*(2), 308–314.

20 Hill, R. A., & Barton, R. A. (2005). Red enhances human performance in contests. *Nature, 435*, 293.

21 Hagemann, N., Strauss, B., & Leißing, J. (2008). When the referee sees red . . . *Psychological Science, 19*(8), 769–771.

22 Slepian, M. L., Ferber, S. N., Gold, J. M., & Rutchick, A. M. (2015). The cognitive consequences of formal clothing. *Social Psychological and Personality Science, 6*(6), 661–668.

23 Kraus, M. W., & Mendes, W. B. (2014). Sartorial symbols of social class elicit class-consistent behavioral and physiological responses: A dyadic approach. *Journal of Experimental Psychology: General, 143*(6), 2330.

24 Dress for Success. https://dressforsuccess.org/

25 Barthes, R. (1983). *The fashion system*, trans. M. Ward and R. Howard. New York: Hill and Wang, 1968. Lurie, A. (1992). *The language of clothes* (1st ed. revised). London: Bloomsbury Publishing.

26 McCracken, G. D., & Roth, V. J. (1989). Does clothing have a code? Empirical findings and theoretical implications in the study of clothing as a means of communication. *International Journal of Research in Marketing, 6*(1), 13–33.

27 Boultwood, A., & Jerrard, R. (2000). Ambivalence, and its relation to fashion and the body. *Fashion Theory, 4*(3), 301–321.

28 Shannon, C. E., Weaver, W., & Burks, A. W. (1951). *The mathematical theory of communication*. Urbana, IL: University of Illinois Board of Trustees.

29 Eco, U. (1977). Semiotics of theatrical performance. *The Drama Review: TDR, 21*(1), 107–117.

30 Goffman, E. (1979). Footing. *Semiotica, 25*(1–2), 1–30.

31 Lurie, A. (1992). *The language of clothes* (1st ed. revised). London: Bloomsbury Publishing.

32 Flugel, I. (1930). On the significance of names. *Psychology and Psychotherapy: Theory, Research and Practice, 10*(2), 208–213.

33 Solomon, M. R. (1985). *Psychology of fashion*. Lanham, MD: Lexington Books. Solomon, M. R., & Rabolt, N. J. (2004). *Consumer behavior: In fashion*. Upper Saddle River, NJ: Prentice Hall.

34 Ibid., p. 18.

35 Barnard, M. (2002). *Fashion as communication*. Hove, UK: Psychology Press.

36 Damhorst, M. L. (1990). In search of a common thread: Classification of information communicated through dress. *Clothing and Textiles Research Journal, 8*(2), 1–12.

37 Asch, S. E. (1946). Forming impressions of personality. *Journal of Abnormal and Social Psychology*, 41(3), 258.

38 Goldinger, S. D., Papesh, M. H., Barnhart, A. S., Hansen, W. A., & Hout, M. C. (2016). The poverty of embodied cognition. *Psychonomic Bulletin & Review*, 23(4), 959–978.

39 An animation explaining the concept of enclothed cognition can be found here: https://youtu.be/MtPPaCBJdw0

40 Adam, H., & Galinsky, A. D. (2012). Enclothed cognition. *Journal of Experimental Social Psychology*, 48(4), 918–925.

41 Adam, H., & Galinsky, A. D. (2012). Enclothed cognition. *Journal of Experimental Social Psychology*, 48(4), 918–925.

CHAPTER 7

1 Seligman, M. E. (2002). Positive psychology, positive prevention, and positive therapy. In C. R. Snyder & S. J. Lopez (Eds.) *Handbook of positive psychology* (pp. 3–12). New York: Oxford University Press.

2 Nuffield Council on Bioethics. (2017). *Cosmetic procedures: Ethical issues*. http://nuffieldbioethics.org/project/cosmetic-procedures

3 Eco, U. (1977). Semiotics of theatrical performance. *The Drama Review: TDR*, 21 (1), 107–117.

4 Lurie, A. (1992). *The language of clothes* (1st ed. revised). London: Bloomsbury Publishing.

5 Jiang, E. (2017). Virtual reality: Growth engine for fashion? *Business of Fashion*, 28 February. www.businessoffashion.com/articles/fashion-tech/virtual-reality-growth-engine-for-fashion

Printed in the United States
by Baker & Taylor Publisher Services